IES

Clive Oxenden
Christina Latham-Koenig
Paul Seligson

New
ENGLISH FILE

Elementary
MultiPACK B

Page numbers in this edition are the same as
in the full-length Student's Book and Workbook.

Paul Seligson and Clive Oxenden are the origi
English File 1 (pub. 1996) and *English File 2* (p

OXFORD
UNIVERSITY PRESS

Student's Book Contents

		Grammar	Vocabulary	Pronunciation

Look out for Study Link   This shows you where to find extra material for more practice and revision.

Workbook Contents

5 A

G past simple of *be: was / were*
V word formation: *paint → painter*
P sentence stress

Who were they?

Who was he?
He was a famous musician.

1 LISTENING

a Look at the photo of Mount Rushmore. Who are the men? Match their first names and surnames.

George —— Jefferson
Thomas —— Lincoln
Theodore —— Washington
Abraham —— Roosevelt

b 🔊 **5.1** Listen to an American tour guide. Check your answers.

c 🔊 **5.2** Listen. Complete with numbers and dates.

Guide The second head is of Thomas Jefferson. He was President of the United States from *1801* to _____ .

Tourist 1 When was he born?

Guide He was born in _____ , in Virginia. His parents were very rich.

Tourist 1 Was he President after Washington?

Guide No, he was the _____ President.

Tourist 2 What's Jefferson famous for?

Guide Well, he's famous for writing the Declaration of Independence – that was when he was _____ , before he was President – and for buying the state of Louisiana from Napoleon in _____ .

Mt Rushmore, South Dakota

2 GRAMMAR *was / were*

a Complete the sentences with *was* or *were*.

Present simple	Past simple
The heads **are** of four famous Americans.	They ~~all~~ *were* all Presidents of the USA.
The first head on the left **is** Washington.	He *was* the first American President.

b 🔵 **p.130 Grammar Bank 5A.** Read the rules and do the exercises.

3 PRONUNCIATION sentence stress

a 🔊 **5.3** Listen and repeat. Copy the rhythm.

+ He was <u>born</u> in <u>Virginia</u>. His <u>parents</u> were <u>very rich</u>.
− He <u>wasn't</u> the <u>second President</u>. They <u>weren't all famous</u>.
? <u>Where</u> was he <u>born</u>? <u>When</u> was he <u>born</u>?
  <u>Was</u> he <u>famous</u>? <u>No</u>, he <u>wasn't</u>.
  <u>Were</u> they <u>good Presidents</u>? <u>Yes</u>, they <u>were</u>.

b 🔵 **Communication** *Three Presidents A p.109 B p.112.*
Ask and answer about Washington, Lincoln, and Roosevelt.

c In pairs, ask and answer.

- When were you born?
- Where were you born?
- Where was your mother / father born?
- Where were your grandparents born?

1	2	3	4

The statue of _Nelson_ in _Rome_.

The statue of ~~Gabriel~~ _Garibaldi_ in _Warsaw_.

The statue of _Chopin_ in _Paris_.

The statue of _Joan_ in _London_.

_____ was born in Mazovia in P_____ in 1810. When he was seven years old he was already a brilliant pianist. He was a great composer and his piano music is world-famous and very popular.

_____ was born in 1412 in the village of Domrémy in F_____. She was only a young girl but she was also a soldier and a famous leader in the war against the English.

_____ was born in Norfolk, E_____, in 1758. He was a great sailor. He was famous for his victory against the French at the Battle of Trafalgar in 1805. His statue is in Trafalgar Square.

_____ was born in 1807. His family were from Genoa, in I_____. He was a famous politician and soldier, and a great leader.

4 READING

a Look at the four statues. Who are they? Where are they? Label the photos with the people and cities.

Nelson	Garibaldi	Chopin	Joan of Arc
Rome	Warsaw	Paris	London

b Complete the biographies with the names of the people and the countries they were from.

c **5.4** Listen and check. Cover the texts. What can you remember about the people?

5 VOCABULARY word formation

a You can often make the word for a person by adding an ending to a verb or noun. Look at the examples. What letters do you add?

verb	→	person
paint		painter
act		actor
write		writer

noun	→	person
art		artist
science		scientist
music		musician

b Read the texts again and find the words for people from these verbs and nouns.

1 piano — _pianist_
2 compose (v) — _composer_
3 lead (v) — _leader_
4 sail (v) — _sailor_
5 politics — _politician_

c Underline the stressed syllable and practise saying the words.

d Think of a famous statue of a person in your town, or in the capital of your country. Write a short text about it. Say where it is, who it is, and what the person was famous for.

The statue of _godiva_ *in* _UK_ .
He / She was…

6 SPEAKING

Who was the top British person of all time?

In a BBC survey the winner was Winston Churchill. Other people in the top ten were William Shakespeare, Lord Nelson, John Lennon, and Queen Elizabeth I.

a In groups of three, decide who you think are the top three people of all time from *your* country.

b Tell the class about them.

We think number 1 is _____.
He / She was a famous…

53

5 B

G past simple regular verbs
V past time expressions
P *-ed* endings

> We wanted to go to Sydney.

Sydney, here we come!

1 READING

a **5.5** Read and listen to the true story about Raoul and Emma. Answer the question at the end.

A tale of two Sydneys

Last April two British teenagers wanted to go to Australia for their summer holiday. But it was a 24-hour journey by plane and tickets were very expensive. So, Raoul Sebastian and Emma Nunn, aged 19, looked for cheap tickets on the Internet. They were lucky, and they booked two tickets to Sydney.

On August 4th they arrived at Heathrow airport. They checked in and waited for the plane to leave. Six hours later they landed at a big airport and changed planes.

Emma: 'I was a bit worried because the second plane was very small, but I didn't want to say anything to Raoul.'

Raoul: 'After only an hour the plane landed. We looked out of the window. It was a very small airport. We walked to the information desk and I showed our tickets to the woman.'

'When is our next flight?' I asked.

She looked at our tickets. 'The next flight? This is the end of your journey. Where did you want to go?'

'Where are we?' I asked.

Do you think they were in Sydney?

Adapted from a news website

b Read the story again and number the pictures 1–9.

A 4 B 5 C 7 D 6 E 9
F 4 G 2 H 3 I 1

c **5.6** Listen to the end of the story. Where were they?

d ○ **Communication** *Sydney p.112.* Read about what happened to Emma and Raoul in the end. Is it easy to make a mistake like this?

2 GRAMMAR past simple regular verbs

a Look at the highlighted verbs in the text and complete the chart.

Present simple	Past simple
They want to go to Australia.	They ___went___ to go to Australia.
I don't want to say anything.	I ___didn't___ to say anything.
Where do you want to go?	Where ___did you want___ to go?

b **○ p.130 Grammar Bank 5B.** Read the rules and do the exercises.

c Complete the questions with *Was / Were* or *Did*.
1 ___did___ they want to go to Australia?
2 ___Was___ it a long journey?
3 ___Did___ they book their tickets at a travel agent's?
4 ___Were___ the tickets expensive?
5 ___did___ they check in at Heathrow airport?
6 ___did___ they change planes three times?
7 ___Was___ the second plane big?
8 ___was___ Emma worried?
9 ___did___ the plane land in Australia?
10 ___did___ they stay in Nova Scotia for a long time?

d **5.7** Listen and check. Then listen and repeat. Copy the rhythm.

e In pairs, ask and answer the questions about Raoul and Emma.

Did they want to go to Australia? — Yes (they did).

3 PRONUNCIATION -ed endings

⚠ Past simple regular verbs end in -ed in ⊞ sentences. -ed can be pronounced in three ways.

a **5.8** Listen and repeat the verbs. In which group do you pronounce the *e* in the -*ed*? Why?

1 -ed = /d/	2 -ed = /t/	3 -ed = /ɪd/
arrived	booked	wanted
changed	checked	landed
showed	looked	waited
tried	walked	
	asked	

b **5.9** Listen and repeat Emma and Raoul's story.
1 They wanted to go to Australia.
2 They booked two tickets on the Internet.
3 They arrived at Heathrow airport.
4 They checked in.
5 They landed at a big airport.
6 They changed planes.
7 They looked out of the window.
8 They walked to the information desk.
9 They showed their tickets to a woman.

c Use the pictures in **1b** to re-tell the story from memory. Try to pronounce the past simple verbs correctly.

4 VOCABULARY & SPEAKING

a Number the past time expressions 1–7.

I booked the tickets
yesterday morning.	2
five minutes ago.	1
last November.	5
a year ago.	7
last night.	6
three days ago.	3
last week.	4

⚠ *last April*, NOT ~~the last April~~,
last week, NOT ~~the last week~~
yesterday morning / afternoon / evening
BUT *last night* NOT ~~yesterday night~~

b Stand up and move around the class. Ask *Did you…?* questions. When somebody answers *Yes, I did* write down their name and ask the next question, e.g. *Where to?*

Find a person who…

travelled by plane last year.	_____	Where to?
started learning English a long time ago.	_____	When?
played football last weekend.	_____	Who with?
studied last night.	_____	What?
cooked a meal yesterday.	_____	What?
arrived late for class today.	_____	Why?
listened to the radio this morning.	_____	What programme?
invited a friend to dinner last weekend.	_____	Who?
finished work late last night.	_____	Why?
watched TV last night.	_____	What programme?

Did you travel by plane last year? — Yes, I did.

Where to?

5 C

G past simple irregular verbs
V *go, have, get*
P sentence stress

> Where did you go?
> We went to a restaurant.

Girls' night out

1 VOCABULARY *go, have, get*

a Can you remember? Write *go, have,* or *get*.

~~have~~ lunch   *go* shopping   *get* up

b ⬤ **p.150 Vocabulary Bank** *Go, have, get.*

2 READING

a Do women go out together in your country? Where do they go?

b Look at the photos and read the reports. Where do you think the women are? Write **Rio de Janeiro, Beijing,** or **Moscow.**

© Kong Qingyan, Frederico Mendes, Nikolai Ignatiev/Marie Claire/IPC Syndication

The magazine ***Marie Claire*** asked its women journalists in **Rio**, **Beijing**, and **Moscow** to go out for the evening and then write a report.

	SABINA lives in _____. She went out with her friends Lali and Anna on a Friday night.	**SHARON** lives in _____. She went out with her friends Nicole and Hujia on a Saturday night.
1	I wore a black sweater and trousers and a lot of make-up. Girls here like wearing sexy clothes!	I wore a long dress. People are quite traditional here but young people want to wear new fashions and have new hair colours.
2	We went to Piramida. It's a bar and restaurant that's open 24 hours a day, and it's the 'in' place at the moment. There's a DJ and we saw a lot of interesting people.	First I drove to Bar Street, a street with about 50 bars. We met in the Pink Loft, a Thai restaurant. After dinner we went to a tea house because it's a good place to talk.
3	We had coffee and apple cake and then wine.	We had typical Thai food, like green curry. Then we had tea. Women here don't drink a lot of alcohol.
4	We talked about Lali's problems with her boyfriend. She was a bit sad. Then some men at the next table started talking to us and they bought us a drink. This is a very macho country and men always pay for women's drinks.	We talked about our love lives, especially Hujia's. She has a problem with her partner. We talked about men, fashion, and literature.
5	We got a taxi. It can be quite dangerous here at night and the metro closes at about 12.30.	We went home by car. I didn't drink any alcohol so I could drive.
6	We left Piramida at about 1.30, and I got home at 2.00.	We left at 12.00 and I got home at about 12.30.
7	Fantastic. 10 points. We had a great time and Lali was happy again.	It was a very good night. 8 points.

© Harvey Marcus/Marie Claire/IPC Syndication

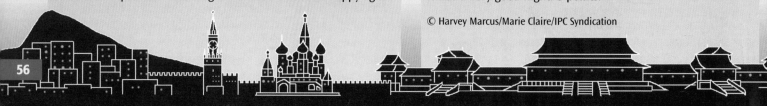

c Match the questions with the women's answers.

Did you have a good time?	☐
How did you go home?	☐
What did you do?	☐
What did you have to eat and drink?	☐
What did you wear?	☐ *1*
What time did you get home?	☐
What did you talk about?	☐

d Read the reports again. Complete the chart with ✓ (= yes) or ✗ (= no).

	Sabina	Sharon
wear a dress?	✗	
go to a bar?		
drink alcohol?		
talk about men?		
talk about clothes?		
go home by taxi?		
get home after 1.30?		

e Compare your answers with a partner. **A** ask about Sabina, **B** ask about Sharon.

Did Sabina wear a dress?

No, she didn't. Did Sharon…?

3 GRAMMAR   past simple irregular verbs

a Look at the reports again and find the past tense of these irregular verbs.

wear	_____	/wɔː/
go	_____	/went/
see	_____	/sɔː/
have	_____	/hæd/
buy	_____	/bɔːt/
get	_____	/gɒt/
leave	_____	/left/
drive	_____	/drəʊv/
meet	_____	/met/
can	_____	/kʊd/

b **5.10** Listen and check. Practise saying the verbs.

c ➲ **p.130 Grammar Bank 5C.** Read the rules and do the exercises.

4 LISTENING

a Look at the third picture in *Girls' Night Out*. Where are they?

b **5.11** Listen to Sílvia talking about their 'girls' night out'. Listen once. Did they have a good time? How many points out of 10?

c Listen again. Answer questions 1–6 from **2c**.

5 SPEAKING & PRONUNCIATION

a Look at the questions below. What words are missing?

b **5.12** Listen and repeat the questions. <u>Copy</u> the <u>rhythm</u>.

A night out

Who / go with?

⇩

What / wear?

⇩

Where / go?

⇩

What / do?

⇩

What / have to eat and drink?

⇩

/ meet anyone?

⇩

How / go home?

⇩

What time / get home?

⇩

/ have a good time?

c Think about the last time you went out with friends. Look at the questions and plan your answers.

d Interview your partner about their night out. Did they have a good time? How many points out of 10?

6   **5.13** SONG ♫ *Dancing Queen*

5
D

G past simple regular and irregular
V irregular verbs
P past simple verbs

Did you hear anything during the night?
No, I didn't. I was very tired.

Murder in a country house

1 READING

a Read the information on the back of the book. What's it about?

MURDER IN A COUNTRY HOUSE

The true story of the murder of a rich businessman. June 22nd 1938 was Jeremy Travers' sixtieth birthday. He had dinner at his country house with his wife, Amanda, his daughter, Barbara, his business partner, Gordon Smith, and his secretary, Claudia Simeone. Next morning when Amanda Travers went to her husband's bedroom she found him in bed … dead.

ISBN 0-19-433846-0

9 780194 338462

b Cover the back of the book and look at the photographs. Can you remember who they are?

Who's Amanda?   She's Jeremy's wife.

Inspector Granger arrived at about 9.00. He was a tall man with a big black moustache. Amanda, Barbara, Claudia, and Gordon were in the living room. The inspector came [1] in.

'Mr Travers died between midnight last night and seven o'clock this morning,' he said [2]. 'Somebody in this room killed him.' He looked at them one by one but nobody spoke [3].

'Mrs Travers. I want to talk to you first. Come into the library with me, please.'

Amanda Travers followed the inspector into the library and they sat [4] down.

'What did your husband do after dinner last night?'

'When we finished dinner Jeremy said he was tired and he went to bed.'

'Did you go to bed then?'

'No, I didn't. I went for a walk in the garden.'

'What time did you go to bed?'

'About quarter to twelve.'

'Was your husband asleep?'

'I don't know, inspector. We… we slept [5] in separate rooms.'

'Did you hear anything when you were in your room?'

'Yes, I heard [6] Jeremy's bedroom door. It opened. I thought [7] it was Jeremy. Then it closed again. I read [8] in bed for half an hour and then I went to sleep.'

'What time did you get up this morning?'

'I got up at about 7.15. I had breakfast and at 8.00 I took [9] my husband a cup of tea. I found [10] him in bed. He was… dead.'

'Tell me, Mrs Travers, did you love your husband?'

'Jeremy is… was a difficult man.'

'But did you love him, Mrs Travers?'

'No, inspector. I hated him.'

138

Jeremy Travers

Amanda

Barbara

Gordon Smith

Claudia Simeone

c **5.14** Read and listen to the story. Mark the sentences T (true) or F (false). Correct the false sentences.

1 Somebody killed Jeremy at 8.00.
2 The inspector questioned Amanda in the living room.
3 Jeremy went to bed before Amanda.
4 Amanda and Jeremy slept in the same room.

5 Somebody opened and closed Jeremy's door.
6 Amanda got up at 7.00.
7 Amanda didn't love Jeremy.

d Look at the ten highlighted irregular verbs in the story. What are the infinitives?

1 *come*

e **○** **p.154 Irregular verbs** and check.

2 PRONUNCIATION past simple verbs

a **5.15** Put these **irregular** verbs in the
correct column. Listen and check.

~~bought~~	came	could	drove
found	had	heard	read
said	sat	saw	slept
spoke	thought	took	wore

	bought						

b **5.16** Find and underline nine past simple **regular** verbs in the story.
How do you pronounce them? Listen and check.

3 LISTENING

a **5.17** Listen to the inspector question Barbara. Write the information in the chart. Listen again and check.

	Amanda	Barbara	Gordon	Claudia
What did they do after dinner?	She went for a walk.			
What time did they go to bed?	11.45.			
Did they hear anything?	Jeremy's door opened and closed.			
Possible motive?	She hated him.			

b **5.18** Listen to the inspector question Gordon. Write the information in the chart.

c **5.19** Listen to the inspector question Claudia. Write the information in the chart.

d Compare your chart with a partner.

e Who do you think was the murderer? Amanda, Barbara, Gordon, or Claudia? Why?

f **5.20** Now listen to what happened. Were you right?

4 SPEAKING

○ **Communication** *Police interview A p.109 B p.112.*
Interview your partner about yesterday.

5 VOCABULARY irregular verbs

○ **p.154 Irregular verbs.** Tick (✓)
the irregular verbs you know. Choose
three new ones and learn them.

A very good way to improve your
English and learn irregular verbs
is by reading Graded Readers.
Buy or borrow a Stage 1 Graded
Reader in the past tense (with a
cassette or CD if possible).

VOCABULARY shopping

a Match the words and pictures.

<u>post</u>cards   ☐ 1

<u>bat</u>teries   ☐ 5

a (<u>ca</u>mera) film   ☐ 2

<u>T</u>-shirts   ☐ 4

a mug   ☐ 3

b In pairs, cover the words and test your partner.

BUYING A PRESENT

a **5.21** Allie is in a gift shop. Cover the dialogue and listen. What does she buy?

YOU HEAR	YOU SAY
Can I help you?	How much is that T-shirt?
1 It's £5 .	Sorry, how much did you say?
£5 .	And how much are those mugs?
2 The big mugs are £4 and the £5 small ones are £6.50 .	Can I have a big mug, please?
3 Sure. there you are. anything else?	Do you have birthday cards?
4 Sorry, *we've only got mugs .	Oh well, just the mug then.
5 That's ok .	Here you are.
6 *Have you got the money ?	Yes, here.
Thanks.	Thank you.
Bye.	Bye.

> * In Britain people often use *I've got* (*I have got*) or *Have you got…?* as an alternative to *I have* or *Do you have…?*

b Listen again. Complete the **YOU HEAR** phrases.

c **5.22** Listen and repeat the **YOU SAY** phrases. Copy the <u>rhy</u>thm.

d In pairs, roleplay the dialogue.

SOCIAL ENGLISH

a **5.23** Listen. Mark the sentences T (true) or F (false).

1 Mark likes Allie's dress.

2 Mark breaks the mug.

3 They get a taxi to the restaurant.

4 Allie reserved a table for 8.30.

b Why is Allie stressed?

c Who says the **USEFUL PHRASES**, Mark or Allie? Listen again and check. How do you say them in your language?

USEFUL PHRASES

Wow! You look great.

I don't believe it!

No problem.

Come on, it's time to go.

Relax.

a Read Alex's questionnaire and report. Which questions does Alex answer in each paragraph?

paragraph 1   questions __1,____

paragraph 2   questions _____

paragraph 3   questions _____

paragraph 4   questions _____

b Plan your report. Answer the questionnaire for your last holiday. Write short notes (not complete sentences).

Questionnaire

Where did you go for your last holiday?

What did you do?

Please tell us your experiences…

1 Where did you go?
To Rome.

2 When did you go there?
Last August.

3 Who did you go with?
My girlfriend.

4 How did you get there?
By plane – British Airways

5 How long did you stay?
A week.

6 Where did you stay?
In a small hotel near the Colosseum.
Nice and quite cheap.

7 What did you do?
During the day: walked around the city, saw famous places, took photos.

At night: went to restaurants — pasta and wine.

8 Did you buy anything?
Yes, painting and shoes.

9 Did you have a good time?
Fantastic – city full of history, special atmosphere, great food.

10 Did you have any problems?
Very hot, difficult to cross the road.

1 I went to Rome last August with my girlfriend. We flew to Rome with British Airways.

2 We stayed for a week in a small hotel near the Colosseum. The hotel was nice and quite cheap.

3 During the day we walked around the city. We saw all the famous places like the Colosseum and St Peter's, and we threw a coin in the Trevi Fountain. We took a lot of photos. At night we went to restaurants and had fantastic pasta and red wine. Our favourite restaurant was in the Piazza Navona. We bought a painting of Trastevere (the old town) and my girlfriend bought some very expensive shoes.

4 We had a great time. Rome is full of history and has a special atmosphere, and Italian food is wonderful. We only had two problems: it was very hot, and it was very difficult to cross the road.

WRITE a report of your holiday. Write four paragraphs. Answer questions 1–10 in the questionnaire.

Read your report carefully. Check spelling, punctuation (CAPITAL letters and full stops), and grammar (are the verbs in the past tense?). Attach a photo if you have one.

GRAMMAR

a Circle the correct sentence, a or b.

    (a) Hi. I'm Susanna. *(circled)*
    b Hi. I Susanna.

1 a They was Presidents of the USA.
    b They were Presidents of the USA. *(circled)*
2 a Where you were born?
    b Where were you born? *(circled)*
3 a Were the tickets expensive? *(circled)*
    b Did the tickets be expensive?
4 a They booked the tickets last April. *(circled)*
    b They book the tickets last April.
5 a They didn't arrive in Australia. *(circled)*
    b They didn't arrived in Australia.
6 a When does the plane landed?
    b When did the plane land? *(circled)*
7 a Had they a good time last night?
    b Did they have a good time last night? *(circled)*
8 a They leaved the bar very early.
    b They left the bar very early. *(circled)*
9 a I didn't see anything. *(circled)*
    b I didn't saw anything.
10 a What time did you go to bed? *(circled)*
    b What time you did go to bed?

b Write the past simple.

    get   *got*
1 study *studied*
2 go *gone*
3 drive *driven*
4 can *could*
5 wait *waited*
6 say *said*
7 think *thought*
8 write *written*
9 stay *stayed*
10 hear *heard*

                  20

VOCABULARY

a people

Complete with *-er, -or,
-ist,* or *-ian.*

    lead *er*

1 act___
2 art___
3 paint___
4 music___
5 scient___

b verb phrases

Complete with *have, go,* or *get.*

    have a shower

1 _____ a good time
2 _____ an e-mail
3 _____ away for the weekend
4 _____ a taxi
5 _____ a drink

c prepositions

Complete the sentences with *by, for, in, out,* or *to.*

    Look *at* the board.

1 We went _____ a walk in the park.
2 I went _____ with my friends on Saturday night.
3 They went home _____ car.
4 What time did you get _____ the restaurant?
5 I was born _____ 1982.

d past time expressions

~~Cross out~~ the wrong expression.

    She phoned him **yesterday** / ~~**the yesterday**~~.
1 She saw him **ago three weeks** / **three weeks ago**.
2 What time did you get up **yesterday morning** / **last morning**?
3 My birthday was **last month** / **the last month**.
4 We watched TV **last night** / **yesterday night**.
5 The concert was **in last April** / **last April**.

                  20

PRONUNCIATION

a <u>Underline</u> the word with a different sound.

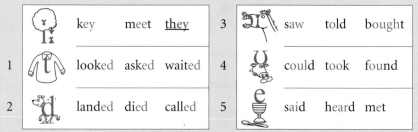

	key	meet	<u>they</u>	3	saw	told	bought
1	looked	asked	waited	4	could	took	found
2	landed	died	called	5	said	heard	met

b <u>Underline</u> the stressed syllable.

infor<u>ma</u>tion

| politician | musician | restaurant | ago | somebody |

                  10

CAN YOU UNDERSTAND THIS TEXT?

a Read the article once and complete the questions with a verb in the past simple.

~~cry~~ ~~go~~ go smoke

First times, Last times

Ben Silverstone in *The Browning Version*.

This week our interview is with Ben Silverstone, a young actor with a great future. His films include *The Browning Version*, *Lolita*, and *Get Real*.

1 When was the first time you _went_ out with a girl?
When I was 12. I took a girl from school to the cinema and then to McDonald's – very romantic! But I didn't have a serious girlfriend until I was 18.

2 When was the first time you _____ a cigarette?
When I was 14. I was in a film called *The Browning Version*. One night after we finished filming I sat with some of the other young actors on the roof of our hotel and I had my first cigarette under the stars. I didn't really enjoy it because I was frightened of falling off the roof.

3 When was the last time you _____ in the cinema?
A long time ago! I don't remember the film. But I remember seeing *Dead Poets' Society* with my father when I was about ten. I thought I was very adult because I didn't cry at the end. Then I looked at my father and he was crying! Very confusing when you're ten years old.

4 When was the last time you _____ to a party?
Last Saturday. It was a barbecue. When summer comes, the English love barbecues in the sun. But as usual it rained, and in the end we ate hamburgers and sausages in the kitchen.

b Read the article again and answer the questions.

1 Was his first date really romantic? Why (not)?
2 Was he inside or outside when he had his first cigarette?
3 Did he cry at the end of *Dead Poets' Society*?
4 Why wasn't the party very good?

c <u>Underline</u> any words or expressions you don't know. Try to guess them from the context. Check with your dictionary. Try to learn *five* new words.

CAN YOU HEAR THE DIFFERENCE?

a **5.24** Listen. Circle a or b.

1 a My mother is a writer.
  b My mother was a writer.
2 a We book tickets on the Internet.
  b We booked tickets on the Internet.
3 a Where do you study English?
  b Where did you study English?
4 a We meet every week.
  b We met every week.
5 a They have a lot of money.
  b They had a lot of money.

b **5.25** Listen. Circle a or b.

1 a He was born in France.
  b He was born in Argentina.
2 a She bought some expensive shoes.
  b She bought some cheap shoes.
3 a He didn't think the film was very good.
  b He thought the film was very good.
4 a They went out on Saturday night.
  b They went out on Friday night.
5 a She got up at 7.00.
  b She got up at 7.30.

CAN YOU SAY THIS IN ENGLISH?

a Can you...? Yes (✓)

☐ say where and when you were born
☐ say five things you did yesterday morning
☐ say five things you did last weekend

b In pairs, choose three questions and ask a partner. Ask for more information.

When was the last time you...?
- saw a film in the cinema
- bought flowers for somebody
- went to a party
- sent a text message
- went away for the weekend
- spent a lot of money

When was the last time you went away for the weekend?

A month ago.

Where did you go?

6 A

G there is / there are
V houses and furniture
P /ð/ and /eə/, sentence stress

Is there a television?
No, there isn't.

A house with a history

1 VOCABULARY houses and furniture

a Order the letters to make three rooms in a house.

chitken _Kitchen_   redboom _bedroom_   thorobam _bathroom_

b Name two things you usually find in these rooms.

c ➲ **p.151 Vocabulary Bank** *Flats and houses*. Do parts 1 and 2.

2 LISTENING

a Read the advert and look at the photo.
Would you like to live in this house? Why (not)?

b **6.1** Larry and Louise are from the USA. They want to rent
the house. Cover the dialogue and listen. Which three rooms in
the house do they go into?

c Listen again and complete the dialogue.

To Rent

Beautiful country
house. Very quiet.
Five bedrooms,
large garden.
Low price.

Estate agent	Well, this is the hall. There are six rooms on this floor. There's a kitchen, a ¹ _bedroom_, a living room, a ² _bathroom_ a library…
Larry	Wow! There's a library, Louise!
Louise	What's that room?
Estate agent	That's a ³ _toilet_ madam.
Larry	How many bathrooms are there?
Estate agent	There's one downstairs and three ⁴ _toilets_
Louise	Are there any ⁵ _bugs_?
Estate agent	No, there aren't, madam. This is an old house.
Estate agent	This is the living room.
Louise	Are those paintings original?
Estate agent	Yes, I think so, madam.
Larry	Is there a ⁶ _Jacuzzi_
Estate agent	No, there isn't, sir. But there's a ⁷ _pool_.
Estate agent	And the kitchen. _fridge_
Louise	There isn't a ⁸ _bar_.
Estate agent	Yes, there is. It's over there,
Louise	You call that a fridge! Are there any ⁹ _ice_? I need a glass of water.
Estate agent	Yes, madam. There are some glasses in that ¹⁰ _cabinet_ Now let's go upstairs.

d **6.2** Larry and Louise and the estate agent go upstairs.
Listen. What problem is there with one of the bedrooms?
Do they decide to rent the house?

64

3 GRAMMAR *there is / there are*

a Read the dialogue in **2c**. Complete the chart.

	singular	plural
+	There's a piano.	There _____ some glasses in the cupboard.
−	There _____ a fridge	There aren't any showers.
?	_____ _____ a TV?	_____ _____ any glasses?

b What's the difference between...?

1 There are **four** glasses in the cupboard.

2 There are **some** glasses in the cupboard.

c ➔ **p.132 Grammar Bank 6A.** Read the rules and do the exercises.

4 PRONUNCIATION /ð/ and /eə/, sentence stress

a **6.3** Listen and repeat. Copy the rhythm.

 A Where's the bathroom?
 B It's upstairs.
 A Is there a lift?
 B No, there are stairs.
 A Where are the stairs?
 B They're over there.

b In groups of three, roleplay the dialogue in **2c** between the estate agent and Louise and Larry.

5 SPEAKING

a Complete the questions with *is there* or *are there*. In pairs, ask and answer.

In your house / flat

1 How many bedrooms _____?
2 How many bathrooms _____?
3 _____ a study?
4 _____ a garden?
5 _____ a garage?
6 _____ central heating?

In your bedroom

7 _____ a TV?
8 _____ any pictures on the wall?
9 _____ any plants?
10 _____ a mirror?
11 _____ any cupboards?
12 _____ a computer?

b Quickly draw a plan of your living room. 'Show' the room to your partner.

> This is the living room. There are two sofas and an armchair...

6 LISTENING

6.4 On their first night in the house, Larry and Louise go to the local pub. Listen and answer the questions.

1 What do they have to drink? Why?
2 What does the barman tell them?
3 What happens in the end?

6

B

G *there was / there were*
V prepositions of place
P silent letters

A night in a haunted hotel

Was there a ghost in the room?

1 VOCABULARY prepositions of place

a Match the words and pictures.

in	2	be<u>tween</u>	7
in front of	6	<u>o</u>pposite	8
on	9	next to	6
<u>u</u>nder	3	over	4
be<u>h</u>ind	1		

1  2

3

4

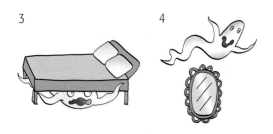

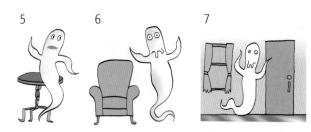

b In pairs, ask and answer with the pictures.

Where's the ghost?   It's under the bed.

c ○ **p.151 Vocabulary Bank** *Flats and houses*.
Play *Where's the ghost?*

2 READING

a Look at the photos and read the introduction below.
Answer the questions.

1 Where is Gosforth Hall Hotel?
2 Who is Stephen Bleach?
3 What is special about Room 11?
4 What did Stephen do?
5 What *couldn't* he do?
6 How did he feel before he went to the hotel?
7 Does he believe in ghosts?

b Do *you* believe in ghosts? Would you like to spend a night
in Room 11 of Gosforth Hall Hotel? Why (not)?

Would you like to spend a night in this room?

THERE ARE MANY old houses, pubs, and hotels in Britain
which people say have ghosts. A British newspaper, the
Sunday Times, sent one of its journalists, **Stephen Bleach**,
to investigate Gosforth Hall Hotel, a small hotel in Cumbria in
the north of England. People say that the hotel has the ghost of a
seventeenth century Catholic priest. The ghost always appears
in Room 11.

Stephen's job was to spend the night alone in Room 11. He
couldn't phone or speak to anybody. Before he went to the hotel,
Stephen said 'I feel a bit nervous, but I don't believe in ghosts.'

GOSFORTH HALL HOTEL
tel **019467 25322**
www.gosforthhallhotel.co.uk
Double rooms **£55**   Room 11 **£65**

c **6.5** Read and listen about Stephen's experience. Label the three pictures with words from the article.

> I arrived at Gosforth Hall late in the evening. It was a very dark night but I could see there was a church with a cemetery next to the hotel. I checked in, and the receptionist gave me the key and showed me to my room.
>
> I left my things in the room and came downstairs. There weren't many guests. There were only three including me. I sat in the sitting room and I talked to the manager, Sara Daniels, about her hotel. I had a drink and then at 12.00 I went upstairs to my room.
>
> Room 11 was on the top floor. I opened the door and turned on the light. It was a very big room, quite old, and yes, it was a bit spooky. There was an old television on a table – but there wasn't a remote control. I turned on the TV. There was a film on. I was happy to see that it wasn't a horror film. I decided to watch the film and have the light on all night. But I was tired after my long journey and after half an hour I went to sleep.

d From memory, correct the information in these sentences. Quickly read the article again to check.

1 There was a cemetery ~~behind~~ the hotel.   *next to*
2 There were three other guests in the hotel.
3 He talked to one of the guests.
4 Room 11 was on the first floor.
5 The room was quite small.
6 There was a horror film on TV.
7 When he went to sleep, the TV and the lights were turned off.

e Do you think Stephen saw the ghost?

3 LISTENING

a **6.6** Listen to Stephen describing what happened. Did he see the ghost?

b Listen again. Complete his report.

Journalist:	Stephen Bleach
The hotel:	Gosforth Hall Hotel
The ghost:	17th century Catholic priest
Did you wake up during the night?	[1] Yes / No
If yes, what time?	[2] _____
Did anything strange happen?	[3] Yes / No
If yes, what?	The [4] _____ and the [5] _____ went off.
Did you see the ghost?	[6] Yes / No
Did you 'feel' the ghost?	[7] Yes / No
Were you frightened?	[8] ☐ very ☐ a little ☐ not at all
Would you like to go back?	[9] Yes / No
Why (not)?	[10] _____

4 GRAMMAR there was / there were

a Complete the sentences from the article with *was*, *wasn't*, *were*, or *weren't*.

1 There _____ many guests in the hotel.
2 There _____ only three including me.
3 There _____ an old TV on a table.
4 There _____ a remote control.

b ➔ **p.132 Grammar Bank 6B.** Read the rules and do the exercises.

5 SPEAKING

➔ **Communication** *Room 11 p.107.*
Look at the picture for one minute. Try to remember what's in the room.

6 PRONUNCIATION silent letters

Some English words have a 'silent' letter, e.g. in *cupboard* /ˈkʌbəd/ you don't pronounce the *p*.

a Practise saying these words. ~~Cross out~~ the 'silent' letter in each one.

g~~u~~est	ghost	half	could	know
building	listen	friend	write	hour

b **6.7** Listen and check.

G present continuous
V verb phrases
P verb + *-ing*

Neighbours from hell

> What are they doing?
> They're having a party.

1 VOCABULARY & SPEAKING

a Read the article about neighbours. Complete the list of problems with these verbs.

argue	bark	cry	have	move	play	talk	watch

Love your neighbour?
Sometimes it can be difficult!

You can choose your friends but you can't choose your neighbours. The people who live upstairs, downstairs, and next door can have a very big influence on our lives – and it isn't always positive! The typical problem that people have with their neighbours is that they make a lot of noise.

In a European newspaper survey these were the top eight problems.

- They _____play music_____ loudly.
- Their babies _____cry_____.
- They _____have_____ noisy parties.
- Their dogs _____bark_____
- They _____watch_____ TV late at night.
- They _____move_____ furniture.
- They _____play_____ a musical instrument.
- They _____argue_____ with their partner.

b In groups of two or three, answer the questions in the survey.

Do you have good neighbours? *yes*
Do you live in a house or a flat? *yes*
What floor do you live on? *55*
Where do you have neighbours? upstairs ☐ downstairs ☐ next door ☑
Do you know your neighbours? *No*
Are they friendly? Do they help you? *yes*
Do they make a lot of noise? What kind of noise? *No*
Do you have any other problems with your neighbours? *No*

2 GRAMMAR present continuous

a Match the sentences with flats 1–8.

He's listening to music. ☐
The baby's crying. ☐
They're having a party. ☐
She's playing the violin. ☐
The dog's barking. ☐
They're arguing. ☐
He's watching football. ☐
They're moving furniture. ☐

b **6.8** Cover the sentences and listen. What's happening? Where?

c Complete the chart.

+	The baby's crying.
	She's playing the violin.
	They're having a party.

−	The baby ___is___ crying.
	She ___is___ _playing_ the violin.
	They ___are___ _having_ a party.

?	___Why's___ the baby _crying_?
	Is ___she___ _playing_ the violin?
	___are___ they _they_ _having_ a party?

d **6.9** Listen and repeat the sentences in the chart. Copy the rhythm.

e ○ **p.132 Grammar Bank 6C.** Read the rules and do the exercises.

f In pairs, point and ask and answer about the people in the flats.

> What's he doing?
> He's watching football. What are they doing?

g **6.10** Listen to the sounds. Write six sentences to say what's happening.

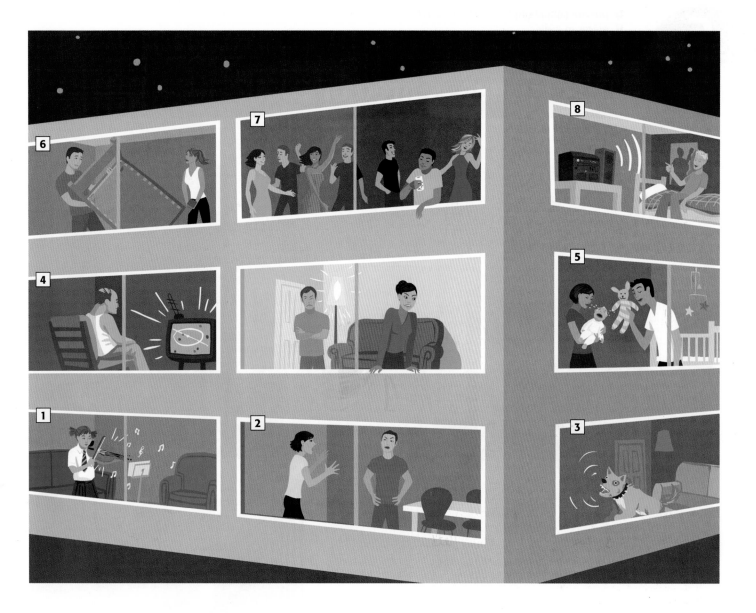

3 PRONUNCIATION verb + *-ing*

a Practise saying the words in the six sound pictures. Then put two words from the box in each column.

🚗 car	🚂 train	🐴 horse	🚲 bike	👢 boot	☎ phone
					smoking

~~smoking~~   dancing   going   playing
asking   calling   doing   moving
talking   crying   driving   raining

b **6.11** Listen and check. Practise saying the words.

c **6.12** Listen to a man on a mobile. Write the six present continuous sentences.

4 SPEAKING

➲ **Communication** *They're having a party!*
A p.110 B p.113. Describe the pictures and find eight differences.

6 D

G present simple or present continuous?
V places in a city
P city names

> Look! The bridge is opening!
> It only opens twice a month.

When a man is tired of London...

1 GRAMMAR present simple or present continuous?

a Look at the photos of four top tourist attractions in London. What are they? Imagine you have one morning in London. Which two would you like to go to?

b **6.13** Where are Ivan and Eva? Cover the dialogues and listen. Number the pictures 1–4.

1 Ivan Look! It͟'s͟ ͟o͟p͟e͟n͟ (open)! A ship ͟l͟e͟t͟'s͟ (go) through!

   Eva We're lucky. The guidebook says that it only _____ (open) two or three times a month!

2 Eva The flag _____ (fly) – that means the Queen is at home. She _____ (not live) here all the time. She often _____ (stay) at Windsor Castle or in one of her other homes.

3 Eva That's Napoleon. He _____ (look) at a model of the Battle of Waterloo.

   Ivan Come on – let's go and see the next room.

   Eva Yes, we _____ (not have) much time. It _____ (close) in twenty minutes.

4 Ivan We _____ (go up)! Wow! Look – there's the Houses of Parliament! And Buckingham Palace over there!

   Eva What a pity it _____ (rain). The guidebook _____ (say) you can see Windsor Castle on a clear day.

c Listen again. Put the verbs in brackets into the present continuous or the present simple. What's the difference between the two tenses?

d ➡ **p.132 Grammar Bank 6D.** Read the rules and do the exercises.

Ivan and Eva are tourists in London

2 READING

a Quickly read the guidebook extract about the London Eye and answer the questions.

1 How high is the London Eye? _____
2 How far can you see on a clear day? _____
3 How many capsules are there? _____
4 How many passengers are there in each capsule? _____
5 How long is the trip? _____
6 How fast does it move? _____
7 What time does it open / close?   In the summer _____
                                     In the winter _____
8 Can you get tickets on the day you want to go? _____
9 Where is the ticket office? _____
10 Which underground station is near the London Eye? _____

The London Eye

The London Eye was opened on New Year's Eve 1999 to celebrate the Millennium. It is 135 metres high, and from the top you can see all of London. On a clear day you can even see Windsor Castle, which is 40 kilometres away. The London Eye has 32 capsules, each with room for 25 people. Each 'trip' lasts 30 minutes. It moves quite slowly, at a speed of about 15 metres a minute, but it never stops. Passengers have to get on when it's moving.

Opening times Daily from 9 a.m. to 10 p.m. in the summer and from 10 a.m. to 6 p.m. in the winter.

Tickets In advance online or by phone. A limited number of tickets are available on the day from the Ticket Office in County Hall (the building next to the Eye), but go early because you often have to queue.

How to get there 5 minutes' walk from Waterloo underground station.

www.londoneye.com

b Match the highlighted words and expressions with their meanings.

1 _____ before you go
2 _____ you can buy them
3 _____ every day
4 _____ to wait in a line
5 _____ space (for people or things)
6 _____ people who are travelling

c Would you like to go on the London Eye? Why (not)?

3 VOCABULARY places in a city

a Is there a building in your town with a very good view? Where is it? What's its name?

b ➲ p.152 **Vocabulary Bank** *Town and city.*

4 SPEAKING

In pairs, answer these questions.

Your town
Tourist information

1 Do you live in a village, town, or city?

2 Do many tourists visit? When do they come?

3 Are there any important tourist areas near where you live?

4 Where you live, is there...? Write the name.
   an interesting museum _____
   a famous street _____
   a beautiful square _____
   a famous bridge _____
   a good art gallery _____
   an old castle _____
   an important church or mosque _____
   a good department store _____
   a good, cheap hotel _____
   a street market _____

5 What are the top three tourist attractions in your town?

5 PRONUNCIATION city names

Place names in the UK and Ireland are sometimes difficult for visitors to pronounce and understand, e.g. *Leicester* /ˈlestə/.

a **6.14** Listen. What are the eight cities?

b Listen again and repeat the city names. Which city names have an /ə/ sound?

c Practise saying the city names.

d ➲ p.157 **Sound Bank.** Look at the spellings for /ə/.

6 **6.15** SONG ♫ *Waterloo Sunset*

VOCABULARY   directions

a Match the words and pictures.

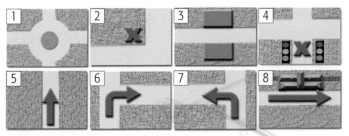

on the <u>co</u>rner ☐	turn left ☐
at the <u>tra</u>ffic lights ☐	turn right ☐
a <u>roun</u>dabout ☐	go straight on ☐
<u>o</u>pposite ☐	go past (*the station*) ☐

b In pairs, cover the words and test your partner.

ASKING FOR DIRECTIONS

a **6.16** Allie and Mark are trying to find the restaurant. Cover the dialogue and listen. Can you mark King Street on the map?

YOU SAY	YOU HEAR
Excuse me. Where's King Street, please?	¹ Sorry, I _____ know.
Excuse me. Is King Street near here?	² King Street? It's _____ here but I don't know exactly _____. Sorry.
Thank you.	
Excuse me. Can you tell me the way to King Street?	³ Yes. Go _____ on. Go past the church, and then turn _____ at the traffic lights. And then I think it's the _____ on the right.
Sorry, could you say that again, please?	Yes, go…
Thank you.	

b Listen again. Complete the YOU HEAR phrases.

c **6.17** Listen and repeat the YOU SAY phrases. Copy the <u>rhy</u>thm.

d In pairs, roleplay asking for and giving directions. **A** ask for the art gallery and the car park, **B** ask for the museum and the station. Start where Allie's car is.

> Excuse me. Can you tell me the way to the art gallery?   Yes, go…

SOCIAL ENGLISH

a **6.18** Listen and complete the sentences.

1 **Allie**   I'm sure she said the _____ on the right.
2 **Mark**   I don't think he knows. He's a _____.
3 **Allie**   Can you see anywhere to _____?
4 **Mark**   Do you think you can park in that _____?
5 **Allie**   Are you saying I _____ park?

b Do they enjoy their dinner?

c Who says the USEFUL PHRASES, Mark or Allie? Listen again and check. How do you say them in your language?

USEFUL PHRASES

Let's ask that man there.
Excuse me! We're lost.
You see. I was right. (opposite = *wrong*)
Here it is.
I'm only joking.

Study Link   MultiROM

a Look at the two postcards. Do you know which city it is?

b Quickly read Melanie's postcard. Which postcard is it?

Dear Kim,

Hope you're OK. We ____ (have) a great holiday here!
We ____ (arrive) four days ago, and we ____ (stay) in
a small hotel in the old town. Yesterday morning we
____ (go) to see the castle, and in the afternoon we
____ (visit) a beer factory.

At the moment we ____ (sit) in a café in the main
square. It's really beautiful. There ____ (be) a
wonderful old clock – you can see it in the picture.

My favourite area is Mala Strana. It's the old part
of Prague and it's fantastic. There ____ (be) a lot of
nice restaurants, and we usually ____ (go) for a walk
there in the evening and then ____ (have) dinner.
You'd really like it.
See you next week!

Love,
   Melanie

PS Matthew sends his love.

Kim Williams

8 Freeman Place

Clifton

Bristol BS4 6MR

England

c Read the postcard again. Put the verbs in the correct form (present simple, present continuous, or past simple).

WRITE a postcard to another student. Imagine you're on holiday in another town or city. Give this information.
- Are you having a good time?
- When did you arrive?
- Where are you staying?
- What did you do yesterday?
- Where are you at the moment?
- What are you doing?
- Say something about the town / city.
- Say what you usually do in the evening.

Check your postcard for mistakes.

GRAMMAR

Circle the correct sentence, a or b.

(a) Hi. I'm Susanna.
b Hi. I Susanna.

1 a There is two tables in the
      living room.
   b There are two tables in the
      living room.

2 a How many bedrooms are there?
   b How many bedrooms there are?

3 a There aren't some glasses.
   b There aren't any glasses.

4 a There were only three guests.
   b There was only three guests.

5 a How many people there were
      in the hotel?
   b How many people were there
      in the hotel?

6 a We having a great time.
   b We're having a great time.

7 a They aren't arguing.
   b They not arguing.

8 a What you are doing?
   b What are you doing?

9 a Look! The bridge opens!
   b Look! The bridge is opening!

10 a The museum closes at 2.00
      on Mondays.
   b The museum is closing at 2.00
      on Mondays.

| 10 |

VOCABULARY

a verb phrases

Match the verbs and phrases.
 have a shower

book	play	have	make	take

1 _____ a noise
2 _____ a musical instrument
3 _____ a party
4 _____ theatre tickets
5 _____ photos

b word groups

Circle the word that is different.

Ireland	(Chinese)	Thailand	Spain

1	kitchen	bathroom	shelf	hall
2	armchair	cooker	sofa	carpet
3	there	behind	opposite	between
4	village	city	town	town hall
5	supermarket	square	bank	chemist's

c prepositions

Complete the sentences with *of, on, to,* or *with.*

   Look _at_ the board.

1 She's arguing _____ her husband.
2 They have their TV _____ very loud.
3 I live _____ the second floor.
4 The TV is in front _____ the cupboard.
5 The table is next _____ the sofa.

| 15 |

PRONUNCIATION

a <u>Underline</u> the word with a different sound.

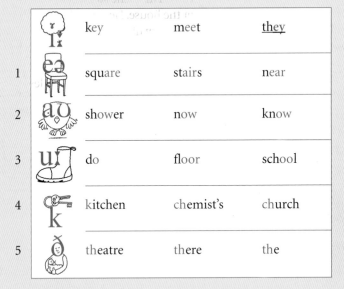

	key	meet	<u>they</u>
1	square	stairs	near
2	shower	now	know
3	do	floor	school
4	kitchen	chemist's	church
5	theatre	there	the

b <u>Underline</u> the stressed syllable.
inform<u>a</u>tion

opposite	between	behind	cupboard	museum

| 10 |

What can you do?

CAN YOU UNDERSTAND THIS TEXT?

Adapted from a British newspaper

Our little piece of pop history

Andrew Holgate and his family bought a house at number 59 Lyndhurst Grove, in London. On their first morning in their new house they were very surprised. They looked out of the window and saw some people taking photographs of their front door. Every week more people came and took photographs. Andrew and his family couldn't understand it. Then they solved the mystery...

The British pop group Pulp have a song on their album *PulpIntro* called *59 Lyndhurst Grove* (written by the singer, Jarvis Cocker). The people who came to see their house were Pulp fans. But why did Pulp sing about 59 Lyndhurst Grove? This is the story. One night Jarvis Cocker came to a party at the house. He argued with the owner, an architect, and the owner threw him out of the house. Jarvis went home and wrote an angry song about the house, the party, and the architect owner.

There are other pop songs about streets. For example, the Beatles wrote a song about Penny Lane in Liverpool. But what is unusual is that Jarvis Cocker's song gives the number of the house. Fortunately, Andrew and his family are quite happy that their house is famous.

a Read the article. Number the sentences in order.

A Jarvis wrote a song about the house. ☐
B Jarvis Cocker went to a party. ☐ 1
C The Holgates found out about the song. ☐
D Andrew's family bought the house. ☐
E The owner of the house threw Jarvis out. ☐
F Jarvis argued with the owner of the house. ☐
G Andrew's family saw people taking photos of the house. ☐

b Read the article again. Mark the sentences T (true) or F (false).

1 There aren't many songs about houses.
2 Jarvis wrote the song because he liked the house.
3 Andrew doesn't like people taking photos of his house.

c <u>Underline</u> five words you want to learn in the text.

CAN YOU HEAR THE DIFFERENCE?

a **6.19** Listen. Circle a or b.

1 How far is the house from Cambridge?
  a 30 miles   b 13 miles
2 How many bathrooms are there?
  a two   b three
3 How old is it?
  a 19 years   b 90 years
4 What day can she see the house?
  a Tuesday   b Thursday
5 What time can she see the house?
  a at 5.45   b at 6.15

b **6.20** Listen. Circle a or b.

1 a There were five guests at the hotel.
  b There were seven guests at the hotel.
2 a Their neighbours are arguing.
  b Their neighbours are watching TV.
3 a Jim is at his friends' house.
  b Jim is at a restaurant.
4 a Maria usually reads in English.
  b Maria doesn't usually read in English.
5 a The gallery closes at 4.00 on Sundays.
  b The gallery closes at 4.00 every afternoon.

CAN YOU SAY THIS IN ENGLISH?

a Can you...? Yes (✓)

☐ say what rooms there are in your house
☐ say what there is in your bedroom
☐ say what you think people in your family are doing now

b Re-order the words to make questions.

1 TVs house are there in many your
  How _____?
2 on was last TV there night
  What _____?
3 computer there your in a bedroom
  Is _____?
4 banks time in the do your open country
  What _____?
5 you today wearing are
  What _____?

c In pairs, ask and answer.

G a / an, some / any
V food, countable / uncountable nouns
P the letters ea

> Is there any beer?
> No, but there's some orange juice.

What does your food say about you?

1 VOCABULARY food

a Look at the picture. Write the missing letters.
What did Laura have to eat and drink yesterday?

> She had an apple, ...

b Food words are countable or uncountable.
Write the words in the correct column.

countable nouns (singular or plural)	uncountable nouns (singular)
an apple	*some butter*
1 9 8 2 5 4	3 6 10 7

c ⊙ p.153 Vocabulary Bank *Food*.

1 an _a_ pple
2 a _b_ anana
3 some _B_ utter
4 an _E_ gg
5 some ___eat
6 some ___ice
7 some ___ugar
8 a ___omato
9 a ___iscuit
10 some ___offee

2 GRAMMAR a / an, some / any

a In pairs, ask and answer.

1 How often do you go to the supermarket?
2 Which supermarket do you go to? Why?
3 Do you look at the food other people are buying?
Does it say anything about them?

b Match the people with the baskets.

Fast Food Frank 3   Healthy Hannah 1   Luxury Lucy 2

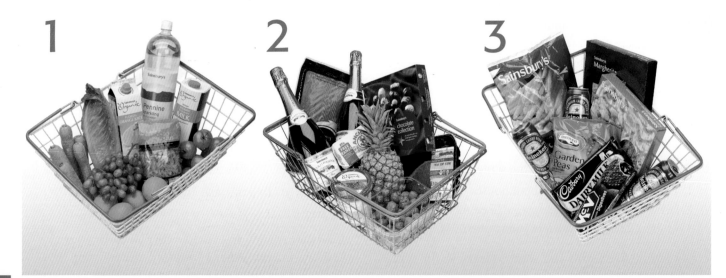

1   2   3

c Read the sentences. Which basket is it? Circle 1, 2, or 3.

a There's **some** ice cream. 1 ② 3
b There isn't **any** fruit. 1 2 ③
c There aren't **any** vegetables. 1 ② ③
d There are **some** biscuits. 1 2 ③
e There's **a** lettuce. ① 2 3
f There isn't **a** pineapple. ① 2 ③

d Look at the sentences and complete the rules with *some*, *any*, or *a / an*.

Use _____ with singular countable nouns, e.g. *pineapple*
Use _____ (+) and _____ (− and ?)
    with plural nouns, e.g. *vegetables*
    with uncountable nouns, e.g. *cheese*

e ▸ **p.134 Grammar Bank 7A.** Read the rules and do the exercises.

f In pairs, A say + and − sentences about the baskets. B say which basket it is. Change roles.

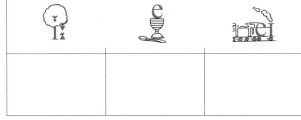

There are some strawberries. — Basket 2.
There isn't any water. — Baskets 2 and 3.

3 PRONUNCIATION the letters *ea*

a How is *ea* pronounced in these words? Put them in the correct column.

| bread | breakfast | eat | health |
| ice cream | meat | peas | steak | tea |

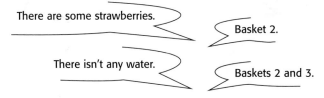

b 🔊 **7.1** Listen and check. Practise saying them. Which is the most common pronunciation of *ea*?

4 SPEAKING

a Make a food diary for yesterday. Write down exactly what food and drink you had. Use **Vocabulary Bank** *Food p.153* to help you.

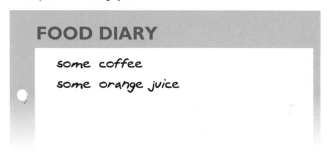

FOOD DIARY

some coffee
some orange juice

b In pairs, A tell B exactly what food you had. B say if you think A is like Fast Food Frank, Healthy Hannah, or Luxury Lucy. Then change roles.

5 LISTENING

a Can you make spaghetti bolognese? What do you need to make it?

CAN MEN COOK?

b 🔊 **7.2** Listen to a TV cooking programme. What nine things does Colin use to make spaghetti bolognese?

1 *some spaghetti* _____
  2 an _____
   3 some _____
    4 a _____
  5 some _____
 6 some _____
  7 some _____
   8 some _____
   9 some _____

c Listen again and check. Does Belinda like Colin's spaghetti bolognese?

d In pairs, think of a famous dish from your country. Write the ingredients you need. Tell the class.

7 B

G *how much / how many?*, quantifiers: *a lot, not much,* etc.
V drinks
P /w/, /v/, and /b/

How much water do you drink?
Not much.

How much water do we really need?

1 PRONUNCIATION /w/, /v/, and /b/

a *7.3* Listen and repeat the sounds and words.

water   vodka   beer

b *7.4* Listen and practise the dialogue.

V Would you like a beer, Bill?
B No, thanks, Vicky. A whisky and water.
V Do you want some biscuits or a sandwich?
B A sandwich.
V Brown bread or white bread?
B Brown bread. It's very good for you.

2 SPEAKING

a Read the introduction and the questionnaire.

b In pairs, interview your partner. Who drinks more water?

3 GRAMMAR *how much / how many?*, quantifiers

a Complete the questions with *How much* or *How many*.

1 _How many_ litres of water do you drink?
2 _____ mineral water do you drink?

b Match the sentences and pictures.

1 I **don't** drink **any** water.	☐
2 I **don't** drink **much** water.	☑
3 I drink **quite a lot of** water.	☐
4 I drink **a lot of** water.	☐

A   **B**   **C**   **D**

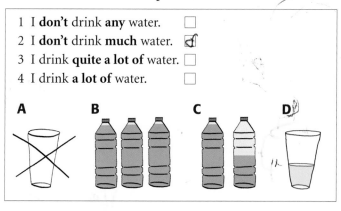

c ➲ **p.134 Grammar Bank 7B.** Read the rules and do the exercises.

How much water do YOU drink?

What do many people take with them everywhere these days? A bag? A mobile? A credit card? Yes, but also a bottle of mineral water. In magazines today there are many articles telling us that we need to drink a lot of water to be healthy and beautiful.

1 How much water do you drink a day?
  a I drink a lot of water. (2+ litres)
  b I drink quite a lot of water. (1–2 litres) ✓
  c I don't drink much water. (0–1 litre)
  d I don't drink any water. (0)

2 When do you drink water?
  a Very often. ✓
  b Only with my meals.
  c Hardly ever.

3 What kind of water do you drink?
  a Only mineral water.
  b Only tap water. ✓
  c Mineral water and tap water.

4 Do you think water is…?
  a healthy but boring ✓
  b healthy and nice
  c perfect when you're thirsty ✓

5 Do you think you need to drink more water?
  a Yes.
  b No. ✓
  c I don't know.

d Complete the questions with *How much* or *How many*.

1	How many	cups of coffee	
2		milk	
3		glasses of wine	
4		cups of tea	do you
5		fruit juice	drink a day?
6		beer	
7		mineral water	
8		Coke	

A lot.

Quite a *lot*.

Not much/many.

None.

e In pairs, ask and answer. Answer with an expression from **d** or a number.

> How many cups of coffee do you drink a day?

> Not many – two or three.

4 READING

a Cover the magazine article *Water – facts and myths*. In pairs, look at these questions. Can you answer any of them?

1 **Why do we need to drink water?**
2 **Do people need less water when the weather's cold?**
3 **Can we drink too much water?**
4 **Can we get the water we need from other drinks or food?**
5 **How much water do we need to drink a day?**
6 **Do Coke and coffee make us dehydrated?**

b Read the article. Put the questions in **a** in the gaps.

c Read the article again. Match the highlighted words with these phrases.

1 _____ how hot or cold it is
2 _____ when water comes out of your body when you are hot
3 _____ scientists do these
4 _____ not a long time ago
5 _____ things people believe which are not true
6 _____ a minimum of
7 _____ have in it
8 _____ the truth is

d Look at the questions in **a** again. In pairs, answer them from memory.

e Is there anything in the article you don't agree with?

Water
– facts and myths

A Why do we need to drink water?

We all know that our bodies need water. Water cleans our body, controls our temperature, and helps to keep us healthy. About 70% of our body is water.

B _____

We often read that we need to drink at least eight glasses of water a day (about two litres). The idea probably came from mineral water companies! In fact, how much water we need depends on the weather and on what we're doing. When we are hot, or if we do sport or exercise, we need to drink more. Some experts say that, in normal conditions, we only really need about one litre a day.

C _____

No. When temperatures are very low we also need to drink more than on a normal day. This is because we wear a lot of clothes so we sweat a lot and lose water.

D _____

Yes, of course. We get water from food, especially fruit and vegetables (an apple is 85% water, an onion is 87%). We can also get water from other drinks like fruit juice, coffee and colas, which contain a lot of water.

E _____

No. In experiments in America some people drank only water and other people drank water, cola, and coffee. Their levels of hydration were more or less the same.

F _____

Yes. It can be dangerous to drink a lot of water. Recently a British actor nearly died after drinking eight litres of water a day for several months.

7 C

G *be going to* (plans)
V holidays
P sentence stress

> What are you going to do?
> We're going to see the sights.

Changing holidays

1 READING

Read about this TV programme. What's it about?

Tonight's TV Don't miss…

Changing Holidays 8.30 p.m.

★ ★ ★ ★

In this new holiday programme we ask two couples to plan their holiday for the same week. Then these two couples change holidays – they go on the holiday the other couple planned! But they don't know where the holiday is until the last moment…

Tonight's couples are Lisa and Jon, and Jerry and Sue.

Lisa   Jon   Jerry   Sue

2 GRAMMAR *be going to* (plans)

a 🔊 **7.5** The presenter from *Changing Holidays* calls Lisa Carter. Cover the dialogue. Listen. What are Lisa and Jon's holiday plans?

b Listen again and complete the dialogue.

Couple 1	Lisa and Jon

Lisa Hello?
Peter Hi! Lisa? This is Peter Douglas from *Changing Holidays*.
Lisa Oh! Hello!
Peter Lisa, what are your holiday plans for next week?
Lisa Er… I'm going to ¹ *fly* to New York with my boyfriend, Jon.
Peter Great. And where are you going to ² _____ ?
Lisa We're going to ³ _____ in the Hotel Athena in Manhattan.
Peter What are you going to ⁴ _____ in New York, Lisa?
Lisa We're going to ⁵ _____ – the shops in New York are fantastic – and in the evening we're going to ⁶ _____ clubbing and ⁷ _____ a show on Broadway.
Peter Are you going to ⁸ _____ the sights too?
Lisa Oh yes, we want to see the Empire State Building, the Statue of Liberty, Central Park…
Peter Well, Lisa, say goodbye to New York. Because we're going to ⁹ _____ your holiday!

c Underline the examples of (*be*) *going to* in the dialogue.
  1 What form is the verb after *going to*?
  2 Do we use *going to* to talk about the past, the present, or the future?

d 🔘 **p.134 Grammar Bank 7C.** Read the rules and do the exercises.

e 🔊 **7.6** Listen to Peter Douglas calling Jerry Harte and complete the chart.

Couple 2	Jerry and Sue
1 Where / go?	
2 Who / with?	
3 How / get there?	
4 What / do?	
5 Where / stay?	

3 PRONUNCIATION sentence stress

a 🔊 **7.7** Listen and repeat Peter's questions in **e**. Copy the rhythm.

b In pairs, use the chart in **e** to roleplay the dialogue between Peter and Jerry.

> Where are you going to go?

> We're going to go to Norway.

4 LISTENING & READING

a **7.8** Listen. The two couples are at the airport. Peter is going to tell them where their holidays are. Are they happy? Why (not)?

b Read the two couples' holiday diaries for the first three days. Are they happy?

MONDAY

It's raining and it's cold. Today we met the other people on the work camp – they're friendly but they're very different from us. Dinner was a disaster – we can't cook.

TUESDAY

We got up at 6.00 and started cleaning the river. In the afternoon we planted 20 trees. It's still raining and all our clothes are wet and dirty.

Lisa and Jon in Norway

WEDNESDAY

This morning the sun came out!! We had the morning free and we went on a boat trip – we stopped work and relaxed! In the afternoon – back to work. And it started raining again.

MONDAY

The hotel's OK but there's no view.

In the morning we went shopping – but we didn't buy anything. In the afternoon we went up the Empire State Building – a great view from the top…

TUESDAY

We like the food very much – there are so many different restaurants. We walked in Central Park – really beautiful. In the afternoon we went to the Guggenheim Museum – incredible.

Sue and Jerry in New York

WEDNESDAY

Today was a great day. We saw the sights – Brooklyn Bridge, the Statue of Liberty. In the evening we went to The Village, a famous nightclub – we went to bed at 3 a.m.!

c **7.9** Listen to the end of the programme. Did they have a good time? Where are they going to go next year?

d Listen again. Tick (✓) what they liked, cross (✗) what they didn't like.

Lisa and Jon				Jerry and Sue			
the work	✗	the weather	☐	the hotel	☐	the food	☐
camping	☐	going to bed early	☐	the sights	☐	the nightlife	☐
the people	☐			the people	☐		

5 SPEAKING

Play *Changing Holidays.*

a In pairs, plan your ideal summer holiday. Decide…

- where / go?
- how / get there?
- where / stay?
- what / do there?

OK. Where are we going to go?

Why don't we go to…?

That's a good idea.

b Write down your plans. Give them to your teacher. He / She is going to 'change your holiday'.

c Look at your new holiday. Work with another pair. Ask about their new holiday. Use the questions in **a**. Ask *Are you happy with your new holiday? Why (not)?*

6 **7.10** SONG ♫ *La Isla Bonita*

7 D
G *be going to* (predictions)
V verb phrases
P /ʊ/, /uː/, and /ʌ/

> You're going to be very happy.

It's written in the cards

1 READING & LISTENING

a Match the cards and verb phrases.

- **J** be <u>fa</u>mous
- **I** get a new job
- **h** get <u>mar</u>ried
- **E** fall in love
- **c** <u>tra</u>vel
- **D** get a lot of <u>mo</u>ney
- **G** have a sur<u>prise</u>
- **A** be <u>luc</u>ky
- **F** move house
- **B** meet <u>some</u>body new

b 🔊 **7.11** Cover the story. Read and listen to the first paragraph only. In pairs, answer the questions. Then do the same with the other four paragraphs.

It's written in the cards

'Come in,' said a voice. Jane Ross opened the door and went into a small room. There was a man sitting behind a table.

'Good afternoon,' said Jane. 'I want to see Madame Yolanda, the fortune teller.'

'Madame Yolanda isn't here today,' said the man. 'But don't worry. I'm going to tell you about your future. What questions do you want to ask?' Jane looked at the fortune teller. She couldn't see him very well because the room was very dark.

1 Who does Jane want to see?
2 Who is going to tell her about her future? Why?
3 Why can't she see the man very well?

🔊 **7.12**

Well,' she said, 'I have a problem with my boyfriend. We argue all the time. I don't think he loves me. I want to know if we're going to stay together.'

'Please choose five cards, but don't look at them.'

Jane took five cards. The fortune teller put them on the table face down. He turned over the first card.

'Ah, this is a good card. This means you're going to be very lucky.'

'But am I going to stay with my boyfriend?' Jane asked.

'Maybe,' said the fortune teller. 'We need to look at the other cards first.'

4 What's Jane's problem?
5 How many cards does she take?
6 What is her first card? What does it mean?

He turned over the second card.

'Mm, a house. A new house. You're going to move, very soon, to another country.'

'But my boyfriend works here. He can't move to another country.'

'Let's look at the next card,' said the fortune teller. He turned over the third card.

'A heart. You're going to fall in love.'

'Who with?' asked Jane.

'Let me concentrate. I can see a tall man. He's very attractive.'

'Oh, that's Jim,' said Jane.

'Who's Jim? Your boyfriend?'

'No. Jim's a man I met at a party last month. He's an actor, and he says he's in love with me. It was his idea for me to come to Madame Yolanda.'

'Well, the card says that you're going to fall in love with him.'

'Are you sure?' asked Jane. 'But what about my boyfriend?'

'Let's look at the fourth card,' said the fortune teller.

7 What's the second card? What does it mean?

8 Why is this a problem for Jane?

9 What's her third card? What does it mean?

10 Who's Jim? Where did Jane meet him?

11 What do you think the fourth card is going to be?

The fortune teller turned over a card with two rings.

'Now I can see everything clearly. You are going to leave your boyfriend and go away with the other man, to another country. You are going to get married.'

'Married? But am I going to be happy with him?'

'You're going to be very happy.'

Jane looked at her watch. 'Oh no, look at the time. I'm going to be late.'

She stood up, left a £50 note on the table, and ran out of the room.

12 What is her fourth card? What does it mean?

13 Why is she in a hurry?

14 How much does she pay?

The fortune teller stood up. He turned on the light. At that moment an old woman came in. 'So, what happened?' she asked.

'She believed everything,' said Jim. 'I told you, I'm a very good actor!'

He gave the woman £100.

'That's Jane's £50 and another £50 from me. Thanks very much, Madame Yolanda.'

Madame Yolanda took the money. The fifth card was still on the table, face down. She turned it over. It was the ship. She looked at it for four or five seconds and then she said:

'Young man! Don't travel with that girl – you're going to…'

But the room was empty.

15 Who was the fortune teller?

16 Why does he pay Madame Yolanda £50?

17 What's the fifth card? What do you think is going to happen?

2 GRAMMAR *be going to* (predictions)

a Look at these two sentences. Which one is a *plan*? Which one is a *prediction*?

1 She's going to be very lucky.

2 She's going to go to New York next week.

b ● **p.134 Grammar Bank 7D.** Read the rules and do the exercises.

3 PRONUNCIATION /ʊ/, /uː/, and /ʌ/

a Put these words from the story in the correct column. Be careful, *oo* can be /ʊ/ or /uː/.

good	look	love	lucky	money
move	put	couldn't	argue	you
new	young	but	soon	woman

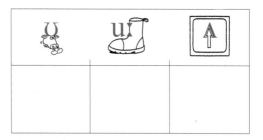

b 7.16 Listen and check.

c ● **p.157 Sound Bank.** Look at the typical spellings for these sounds.

4 SPEAKING

Roleplay fortune telling.

A Look at the ten cards in exercise 1. Secretly, number the cards in a different order.

B Choose five numbers.

A Predict B's future using those cards. Then change roles.

I'm going to tell you about your future. Your first card is a star. You're going to be famous. Maybe you're going to be on TV…

VOCABULARY a menu

a Complete the menu.

> Main **cou**rses   De**sser**ts
>
> **Star**ters

b What do the highlighted words mean? How do you pronounce them?

c Cover the menu. In pairs, try to remember what's on the menu.

Donatella's

_____
Onion soup
Goat's cheese salad

_____
Steak and chips
Roast chicken with vegetables
Fresh lasagne

_____
Home-made vanilla ice cream with hot chocolate sauce
Fresh fruit salad
Tiramisu

2 courses £15.00
3 courses £22.50

ORDERING A MEAL

a **7.17** Allie and Mark are having dinner. Cover the dialogue and listen. What do they order?

YOU HEAR	YOU SAY
¹ Good _____. Do you have a reservation?	**A** Yes, a table for two. My name's Allie Gray.
² _____ or non-smoking?	**A** Non-smoking, please.
³ Come this _____, please.	
⁴ Are you _____ to order?	**M** Yes, I'd like the onion soup and then the steak, please.
	A The goat's cheese salad and the lasagne for me, please.
⁵ What would you like to _____?	**M** Would you like some wine?
	A No, thanks. Just mineral water for me.
	M OK. A glass of red wine and a bottle of mineral water, please.
Thank you, sir.	**M** Thank you.

b Listen again. Complete the YOU HEAR phrases.

c **7.18** Listen and repeat the YOU SAY phrases. <u>Copy</u> the <u>rhythm</u>.

d In groups of three, use the menu to roleplay ordering a meal. **A** is the waiter, **B** and **C** are customers.

SOCIAL ENGLISH

a **7.19** Listen and answer the questions.

1 What do they order for dessert / coffee?
2 What does Mark ask Allie?
3 What does she answer?
4 What does Mark ask the waiter at the end?

b What do you think?

1 Why does Mark want Allie to go to the conference?
2 Is Allie going to say yes?

c Who says the USEFUL PHRASES, Mark or Allie? Listen again and check. How do you say them in your language?

USEFUL PHRASES

It was delicious.
What is there?
Nothing for me, thanks.
The same for me, please.
I'm not sure.
Could we have the bill, please?

Luxury Lucy's favourite sandwich

a Match the ingredients and pictures.

You need:

☐ some brown bread

☐ some smoked salmon

☐ some cream cheese

☐ a lemon

☐ some black pepper

b Read the instructions. Complete them with *cut* or *put*.

1 First _slice_ two thin pieces of brown bread.

2 Then _add_ some cream cheese on one of the pieces.

3 _put_ some pieces of smoked salmon on the cream cheese.

4 _cut_ the lemon in half.

5 _and_ a little lemon juice and black pepper on the salmon.

6 Now ____ the other piece of bread on top.

7 Finally – eat the sandwich! It's delicious!

WRITE instructions to make *your* favourite sandwich.

• Invent a name for it.

• Say what ingredients you need (some bread, etc.).

• Write the instructions.

Check your instructions for mistakes.

GRAMMAR

Circle the correct sentence, a or b.

   (a) Hi. I'm Susanna.
   b Hi. I Susanna.

1 a Are there any onions?
   b Are there an onions?
2 a There's a butter in the fridge.
   b There's some butter in the fridge.
3 a We don't need some bread.
   b We don't need any bread.
4 a How much fruit do you eat a day?
   b How many fruit do you eat a day?
5 a I drink quite a lot coffee.
   b I drink quite a lot of coffee.
6 a She doesn't drink much water.
   b She doesn't drink many water.
7 a I go to buy my ticket today.
   b I'm going to buy my ticket today.
8 a Are they going to get married?
   b Do they going to get married?
9 a What you are going to do
      this summer?
   b What are you going to do
      this summer?
10 a It's going to rain next week.
    b It's going to rain the next week.

| | 10 |

VOCABULARY

a **verb phrases**

Match the verbs and phrases.

get a taxi

get	meet	move	stay	see

1 _____ in a hotel
2 _____ the sights in a city
3 _____ a new job
4 _____ somebody new
5 _____ house

b **food**

Circle the word that is different.

Ireland	(Chinese)	Thailand	Spain
1 breakfast	lunch	dessert	dinner
2 mushrooms	strawberries	onions	peas
3 orange juice	sugar	milk	mineral water
4 crisps	chips	tomatoes	potatoes
5 fruit salad	ice cream	coffee	cake

c **prepositions**

Complete the sentences with *for*, *in*, *of*, *on*, or *with*.

   Look _at_ the board.

1 Is there any water _____ the fridge?
2 I drink a lot _____ coffee.
3 Water is good _____ you.
4 Who are you going to New York _____?
5 They're going to go _____ holiday together.

| | 15 |

PRONUNCIATION

a <u>Underline</u> the word with a different sound.

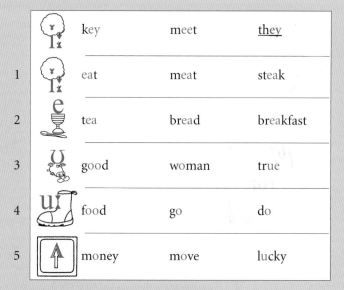

	key	meet	<u>they</u>
1	eat	meat	steak
2	tea	bread	breakfast
3	good	woman	true
4	food	go	do
5	money	move	lucky

b <u>Underline</u> the stressed syllable.

infor<u>ma</u>tion

dessert	menu	vegetables	banana	biscuit

| | 10 |

CAN YOU UNDERSTAND THIS TEXT?

Food can be dangerous for your health!

WHEN you go to a restaurant you often think that the food you are ordering is good for you. But many restaurants serve healthy food, like fish or salad, with a sauce or dressing that uses a lot of oil, fat, or sugar. The British Food Standards Agency wants all restaurants to say in their menus exactly what is in each dish, how many calories, how much fat, and what additives. They think that restaurants don't give their customers enough information, and that this new plan could help people to have a healthier diet.

But chefs are not happy with the Agency's plan. One top chef said, 'People are not stupid. They know that many sauces have butter and cream in them. But if we put on a menu that a dish has 1,000 calories, nobody is going to order it!'

However, many doctors agree with the plan. Bruce Ward, Professor of Medicine, said, 'People know that cigarettes are bad for them, because it tells you on the packet. But when they go to a restaurant they often have no idea if the food is healthy or not. Food products that have a lot of calories, fat, and sugar need a health warning, exactly like cigarettes.'

Adapted from a British newspaper

a Read the article. Circle a, b, or c.

1 Many restaurants…
   a serve healthy food.
   b only serve fish and salad.
   c serve healthy food but with unhealthy sauces.

2 The British Food Standards Agency wants restaurants…
   a to serve healthy food.
   b to give more information about their dishes.
   c not to use fat and additives.

3 Chefs think that…
   a people are not going to order their dishes.
   b people are stupid.
   c cream and butter are good for you.

4 Doctors think that people…
   a need more information about cigarettes.
   b need more information about food.
   c need to stop eating in restaurants.

b Read the article again. <u>Underline</u> and learn five new words connected with food or cooking.

CAN YOU HEAR THE DIFFERENCE?

a 〔7.20〕 Listen. Circle a or b.

1 a There's some milk in the fridge.
   b There isn't any milk in the fridge.
2 a The woman doesn't drink much coffee.
   b The woman drinks a lot of coffee.
3 a She's going to go to Australia.
   b She's going to go to Italy.
4 a They're going to go to a restaurant.
   b They're going to go to the cinema.
5 a She thinks they're going to get married.
   b She doesn't think they're going to get married.

b 〔7.21〕 Listen to a woman shopping. Answer the questions.

1 What does she buy? Tick (✓) the boxes.

carrots	☐	oranges	☐
peas	☐	onions	☐
strawberries	☐	tomatoes	☐
grapes	☐	mushrooms	☐

2 How much does she pay?

CAN YOU SAY THIS IN ENGLISH?

a Can you…? Yes (✓)

☐ say five things that there are in your fridge

☐ say three *healthy* things that you eat or drink a lot of

☐ say three *unhealthy* things that you eat or drink a lot of

b In pairs, ask and answer questions about your plans.

Tonight	Next weekend
/ study English?	/ go away?
What / have for dinner?	/ stay at home
What / do after dinner?	on Saturday night?

Tomorrow	Next summer
What time / get up?	/ go abroad?
Where / have lunch?	Where / go?
What / do in the evening?	

Are you going to study English tonight?

G comparative adjectives
V personality adjectives
P /ə/, sentence stress

8A The True False Show

Yellow cars are safer than white cars.

1 SPEAKING & LISTENING

THE TRUE FALSE SHOW

1	Mosquitoes are more dangerous than sharks.
2	Brown eggs are healthier than white eggs.
3	The Earth is hotter than Mars.
4	Coffee is more popular than tea in the UK.
5	Tigers are better swimmers than cats.
6	An adult is shorter in the morning than in the evening.
7	White cars are safer than yellow cars.
8	The word 'yes' is more common than the word 'no'.

a Look at the pictures. What can you see?

b In pairs, look at the sentences from *The True False Show*. Write T (true) or F (false).

c **8.1** Listen to *The True False Show*. Check your answers. How much money does Darren win?

2 GRAMMAR comparative adjectives

a Look at the adjectives in the quiz sentences. In pairs, answer the questions.

Using adjectives to compare two things:

1 What two letters do you put at the end of one-syllable adjectives (e.g. *short*)?
2 Why is *hot* different?
3 What happens when an adjective ends in *-y*?
4 What word do you put in front of long adjectives (e.g. *popular*)?
5 What's the missing word?
China is bigger ___than___ Japan.

b ⊙ **p.136 Grammar Bank 8A.** Read the rules and do the exercises.

3 PRONUNCIATION /ə/, sentence stress

a `8.2` Listen and repeat the comparative adjectives. Underline the stressed syllable. How is *-er* pronounced at the end of a word?

healthier
hotter
better
shorter
safer

b `8.3` Listen and repeat the eight quiz sentences from 1b. Copy the rhythm.

c ⊙ **Communication** *True False Show A p.110 B p.113.* Write eight quiz sentences. Then play *The True False Show.*

4 VOCABULARY personality adjectives

Match the adjectives of personality with their meaning.

aggressive   careful   stylish   ~~friendly~~
generous   quiet   serious

1 a _friendly_ person is open and kind
2 a _careful_ person doesn't make mistakes or have accidents
3 a _serious_ person thinks a lot and doesn't make jokes
4 a _quiet_ person doesn't talk a lot
5 a _generous_ person likes giving people things ✓
6 a _stylish_ person dresses well
7 an _aggressive_ person likes arguing and can be violent

5 LISTENING

a What colour is your / your family's car? Do you like the colour?

b `8.4` You're going to listen to a radio programme about car colours and personality. Listen once and write the colours in the chart.

your car colour	your personality
1 _yellow_	very _fun_ (more popular with women than men)
2 _white_	_____ (very popular with doctors)
3 _black_	more _____ than normal
4 _____	_____
5 _____	_____
6 _____	_____ (popular with business people)
7 _____	_____

c Listen again and complete 'your personality' with the adjectives from 4.

d Think of three people you know who have a car. What colour are their cars? Is their personality the same as in the chart?

8
B
G superlative adjectives
V the weather
P consonant groups

The highest city in the world

What's the coldest place in the world?

1 READING

a Look at the photos. Where do you think the places are?

b Read the article and complete each heading with a phrase.

The coldest **The highest** **The hottest**

EXTREME LIVING

Welcome to the coldest, highest, and hottest places in the world!

_____ **country in the world**

How do people live in **Mali**, West Africa, where the temperature is often 50°? John Baxter, a BBC journalist in Mali, says, 'People get up very early and they don't move very much in the afternoon. Surprisingly, they wear a lot of clothes (usually cotton) as this helps them not to get dehydrated. Houses are very hot and don't have air conditioning – the best place to sleep is on the roof!'

c Read the article again. Answers these questions.

1 Where do people wear a lot of cotton clothes? _____Mali_____
2 Where is a good place to play golf? _____La paz_____
3 Where do people sleep on the roof? _____
4 Where can you have a problem with your nose? _____
5 Where do you need to be careful in spring? _____
6 Where is a bad place to drink a lot of alcohol? _____

d In pairs, guess the meaning of the highlighted words. Check with your teacher or a dictionary.

e Choose five new words to learn from the article.

_____ **capital city in the world**

La Paz in Bolivia is 4,090 metres above sea level . It can be difficult to breathe because there isn't much oxygen. Liz Tremlett, a travel agent who lives there, says, 'When people arrive at El Alto airport we sometimes need to give them oxygen.' It is also the worst place to be if you drink too much beer. The next day you feel terrible because you get more dehydrated. But La Paz is a very good place to play golf. At this altitude , when you hit a golf ball it goes further!

_____ **place in the world**

Can you imagine living in a place which is four times colder than your freezer ? This is **Yakutia** in Siberia, where in winter it is often −50° or lower. Valeria Usimenko, a housewife, says, 'After a few minutes outside your nose fills with ice. It snows a lot and there is always a lot of ice and snow on top of the houses. The most dangerous time is the spring – when the ice falls it can kill people! The winter is very boring because we can't go out much. A lot of babies are born here in the autumn!'

Adapted from a magazine

2 GRAMMAR superlative adjectives

a Complete the chart with superlatives from the article.

adjective	comparative	superlative
cold	colder	_the coldest_
high	higher	the higest
hot	hotter	the hottest
dangerous	more dangerous	_____
good	better	_____
bad	worse	_____

b ○ **p.136 Grammar Bank 8B.** Read the rules and do the exercises.

3 PRONUNCIATION consonant groups

a **8.5** Listen and repeat the adjectives in 2a.

b **8.6** Words which have two or three consonants together can be difficult to pronounce. Listen and repeat these superlatives.

the most expensive   the most beautiful
the most crowded   the smallest
the driest   the fastest
the coldest   the strongest

c Complete the questions with superlative adjectives. Then ask and answer the questions with a partner.

World Capitals Quiz

1 What's the _____ capital city in the world? (noisy)
  a Tokyo   b Madrid   c Rome

2 What's the _____ capital city in the world? (big)
  a Buenos Aires   b Mexico City   c Tokyo

3 What's the _____ capital city in the world? (dry)
  a Nairobi   b Lagos   c Cairo

4 What's the _____ capital city in the world? (expensive)
  a London   b Tokyo   c Washington

5 What's the _____ capital city in the world? (safe)
  a Copenhagen   b Canberra   c Oslo

6 What's the _____ capital city in the world? (crowded)
  a Beijing   b Bangkok   c New Delhi

4 VOCABULARY the weather

a What's the weather like? Match the sentences and pictures.

1 It's raining / wet. ☐
2 It's sunny / dry / hot. ☐
3 It's snowing / cold. ☐
4 It's cloudy. ☐
5 It's windy. ☐

b What's the weather like where you are today?

5 SPEAKING

In pairs or small groups, ask and answer these questions about your country.

What's the wettest place?   I think it's...

How well do you know your country?

climate
What's / wet / place?
What's / hot / place?
What's / windy / place?
What's / cold / place?

geography
What's / high / mountain?
What's / long / river?
What's / big / city?

tourism
What's / beautiful / city?
What's / popular / place for tourists? Why?
What's / good / time of year to visit? Why?
What's / bad / time of year to visit? Why?
What's / good / way to travel round the country?
What's / dangerous / city?

6 **8.7** **SONG** ♫ *The Best*

8 C

G *would like to / like*
V adventures
P sentence stress

> Would you like to fly a plane?
> No, I don't like flying.

Would you like to drive a Ferrari?

1 READING & SPEAKING

a Do you like buying presents? Who's the easiest person in your family to buy presents for? Who is the most difficult?

b Read the advert. Match the *Experience* presents with paragraphs A–F.

Are you looking for
A REALLY SPECIAL PRESENT?

WHSmith's Amazing Adventures are the perfect original present

Do you know somebody who would like to drive a real Ferrari, salsa dance, or fly in a balloon? There are more than 40 'experience presents' to choose from. Each Amazing Adventure comes in an attractive box including a book and video.

---

c Read paragraphs A–F again. Answer these questions.

Which amazing adventure is…?
- the cheapest
- the most expensive

Which do you think is…?
- the most dangerous
- the most exciting
- the most boring
- the most difficult
- the most useful

d Which one…
- would you like as a present? Why?
- would you like to give to someone in your family? Why?

I

EXPERIENCE BALLOONING
GO ON A HOT-AIR BALLOON FLIGHT

2
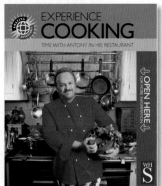

EXPERIENCE COOKING
TIME WITH ANTONY IN HIS RESTAURANT

3
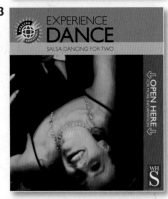

EXPERIENCE DANCE
SALSA DANCING FOR TWO

4

EXPERIENCE TIGER MOTH
GO ON A VINTAGE FLYING LESSON

5

EXPERIENCE FERRARI
DRIVE A FERRARI

6
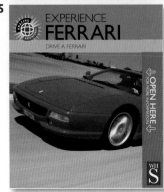

EXPERIENCE STUDIO
RECORD A TRACK AT A PROFESSIONAL STUDIO

A Do you like singing in the shower? Would you like to be a pop star? Now you can record the song of your dreams at a real recording studio. Price £249.99

B Do you like seeing historic cars and planes? Would you like to go back in time and learn to fly an authentic World War II plane?
Price £139.99

* For people of maximum weight 102 kg, maximum height 1.92 m

C Do you like cooking? Would you like to spend a day with a famous chef and learn new recipes and techniques? Then this is the adventure for you. The day includes a delicious lunch (with wine).
Price £149.99

D You like driving fast, but your car is very slow. Now you too can drive this famous Italian sports car.
Price £229.99

* Minimum age 19, with driving licence

E It's easy! It's fun! Everybody's doing it! Wouldn't you like to learn, and be the star of the dance floor?
Price £39.99

F Would you like to have the experience of a lifetime and go up into the sky in a hot-air balloon? The flight lasts about one hour, and the adventure ends with a glass of champagne.
Price £189.99

2 GRAMMAR would like to / like

a Look at the dialogue. In pairs, answer the questions.

A Would you like to learn salsa?

B No, I wouldn't. **I don't like dancing.**
But **I'd like to drive** a Ferrari.

---

1 What's the form of the verb after *would like*?
2 Does *Would you like…?* mean…
   a Do you like…?   b Do you want…?
3 What's the difference between *I like dancing* and *I'd like to dance*?

b ○ **p.136 Grammar Bank 8C.** Read the rules and do the exercises.

3 PRONUNCIATION sentence stress

a **8.8** Listen and repeat the dialogue. <u>Copy</u> the <u>rhythm</u>.

A <u>Would</u> you <u>like</u> to <u>learn</u> to <u>fly</u> a <u>plane</u>?
B <u>No</u>, I <u>wouldn't</u>.
A <u>Why</u> <u>not</u>?
B Because I <u>don't</u> like <u>flying</u>, and I <u>think</u> it's <u>dangerous</u>.

b **8.9** Listen to this dialogue. <u>Underline</u> the stressed words.

A Would you like to drive a Ferrari?
B Yes, I'd love to.
A Why?
B Because I like driving, but my car's very slow.

c In pairs, practise the dialogues.

d In pairs, use the pictures in **1b**.
Ask *Would you like to…? Why (not)?*

4 LISTENING

a You're going to listen to Russell talking about an 'experience present'. Look at the photo. What was the present? Do you think he enjoyed it?

b **8.10** Listen to these phrases. Match them with the pictures.

1 We learned how to land.
2 I sat on the floor and waited.
3 Then the instructor said 'Jump!' and I jumped.
4 Suddenly the parachute opened, and I floated down.
5 One of the people in my group broke his leg.

c **8.11** Listen to the interview with Russell. Did he enjoy the jump? Would he like to do it again? Why (not)?

d Number the sentences 1–9 in the correct order. Listen again and check.

☐	He fell very fast.	☐	He went up in the plane.
☐	He felt fantastic.	☐	He jumped.
☐	He landed.	☐	His parachute opened.
1	He had some classes.	☐	He felt frightened.
☐	He waited to jump.		

93

8
D

G adverbs
V common adverbs
P adjectives and adverbs

> They drive slowly and work hard.

They dress well but drive badly

1 READING & SPEAKING

a Look at these cities. What countries are they in?

Rio de **Janeiro** **Milan** **Tokyo** **Los Angeles**
Barcelona **Sydney**

b Imagine you are going to live in one of these cities. Mark them **E** (easy for me to live in) or **D** (difficult for me to live in). Compare with a partner. Say why.

c Read the article. Where are the three people living? Complete the gaps with cities from **a**.

d Read the article again. Then cover it and try to remember three things about each city. Did anything surprise you?

The inside story

Three people who live abroad talk about their 'new' countries.

Nuria from Spain lives in
barcelona

Driving 8/10 I was surprised – people <u>drive quite slowly</u>. People use their cars for everything. You never see people walking in the street.

Social life 5/10 People don't go out during the week because they work very hard. It's normal to work twelve hours a day and people usually only have one or two weeks' holiday. Work is the most important thing here, more important than family and social life.

People 9/10 People are really nice here. It's easy to talk to them. And in shops the shop assistants are very helpful. They always say 'Have a good day!'

Chic Boutique
Have a good day!

Tokyo
Mónica from Argentina lives in ~~Rio~~

Safety 10/10 There is almost no crime here. You can walk safely in the city late at night. And you can leave things in your car and nobody steals them!

Driving 7/10 People drive carefully, but the big problem is that there aren't any street names. It's impossible to find where you want to go. Even taxi drivers don't know! Also traffic lights are horizontal and they are difficult to see.

People 9/10 They are shy and polite and they speak very quietly. But when they drink some of them change completely! Last Friday night I went out with people from work and we ended up in a karaoke bar. My boss is usually quite serious but he sang 'My Way' very loudly and badly.

2 GRAMMAR adverbs

a Look at these sentences. How do you make an adverb from an adjective?

> **adjectives**
> They are slow drivers.
> They are careful drivers.

> **adverbs**
> They drive slow**ly**.
> They drive careful**ly**.

b Look at the article again. Find and underline nine verb + adverb phrases. Which adverbs don't end in -ly?

c ⬡ **p.136 Grammar Bank 8D.** Read the rules and do the exercises.

d ⬤ **8.12** Listen and say what is happening. Use an adverb.

They're speaking quietly.

Kevin from the UK lives in Rio

Clothes 8/10 Appearance is very important. Everybody dresses well, but especially the men. They are very elegant and wear very stylish clothes. It is easy to see who the British people are here!

Food 9/10 They love food here and it is fantastic! But times are changing. Today many people under 35 can't cook. Supermarkets are full of food now which you can put in the microwave. When I first came to live here there weren't any McDonald's but now they are everywhere.

Driving 5/10 People here are in love with their cars and they drive very fast. Even the nicest people become more aggressive when they drive.

3 PRONUNCIATION adjectives and adverbs

a Underline the stressed syllable in the adjectives.

adjectives	adverbs
aggressive	aggressively
stylish	stylishly
dangerous	dangerously
polite	politely
beautiful	beautifully
quiet	quietly
careful	carefully
complete	completely

b ⬤ **8.13** Listen and check. Repeat the adjectives.

c ⬤ **8.14** Now listen to the adverbs. Does the stress change?

d Practise saying the adverbs.

4 SPEAKING

a In pairs, complete with a country or city (not yours).

They drive dangerously in _Tokyo_
They dress very stylishly in _rio_ .
You can eat very well in _tokyo_
People in _Ireland_ talk loudly.
They play football badly in _total_ . _america_
They work hard in _Spain_
People speak English very well in _England_
People dance beautifully in _____ .

b Compare your sentences with other students. Do you agree?

c What about in *your* country or city? How do people…?

dress work play football talk drive dance speak English eat

VOCABULARY verb phrases

a Match the verbs and phrases.

ask	call	check out	pay	sign	need

1 _I need_ ~~X~~ a hotel
2 _pay_ for the bill
3 _check out_ by credit card
4 _sign_ your name
5 _ask_ help with your luggage
6 _call_ a taxi (*for somebody*)

b In pairs, test your partner.

CHECKING OUT

a **8.15** Mark is leaving the hotel. Cover the dialogue and listen. What does he ask for? What two things doesn't he need?

YOU HEAR	YOU SAY
Good morning, sir.	Good morning. Can I have my bill, please? I'm checking out.
¹ Which room _is_ it?	Room 425.
² _did_ you have anything from the minibar last night?	Yes, a mineral water. Here you are.
³ How _would_ you like to pay?	American Express.
⁴ Thank you. OK. _can_ you sign here, please? Thank you.	
⁵ _would_ you like me to call a taxi for you?	No, thanks.
⁶ _do_ you need any help with your luggage?	No, I'm fine, thanks.
Have a good trip, Mr Ryder.	Thank you.
Goodbye.	Goodbye.

b Listen again. Complete the YOU HEAR phrases.

c **8.16** Listen and repeat the YOU SAY phrases. Copy the rhythm.

d In pairs, roleplay the dialogue.

SOCIAL ENGLISH

a **8.17** Listen. Circle the correct answer.

1 Allie says the traffic is **terrible / horrible**.
2 Mark gets a **taxi / train** to the airport.
3 Allie is going to meet Mark at the **station / airport**.
4 Mark's flight leaves in **30 / 40** minutes.
5 Allie's boss said she **can / can't** go to the conference.

b What do you think is going to happen to Mark and Allie in the future?

c Who says the USEFUL PHRASES, Mark or Allie? Listen again and check. How do you say them in your language?

USEFUL PHRASES

*I'll call a taxi.
Well, thanks for everything.
*I'll meet you (*at the airport*).
Where can we meet?

Could you call me a taxi, please?
Sorry I'm late.
Have a safe trip!

*I'll = I will (future)

Study Link MultiROM

Making a reservation

a Read about the three hotels. Which one would you most like to go to?

Mena House Oberoi Hotel, Giza, Egypt

This hotel is where Egyptian kings stayed! It is a luxury hotel with the best view of the pyramids, and is the only hotel in Egypt with a golf course. Double rooms from € 249.

www.oberoihotels.com

Hotel Danieli, Venice, Italy

This hotel has 91 beautiful rooms. The best rooms are in the old part (ask for Dandolo's palace) and there's a wonderful roof terrace with views over the lagoon. Double rooms from € 349.

danieli.hotelinvenice.com

THE RESIDENCE, TUNIS, TUNISIA

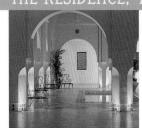

This amazing hotel has a sea water spa and beautiful gardens. Famous guests include Sting and Catherine Deneuve. Double rooms from € 211.

www.theresidence-tunis.com

b Read Sylvie's e-mail. Which hotel is she writing to?

From	Sylvie Vartan sylvievartan@hotmail.com
To	
Subject	Reservation for November

Dear Sir / ¹ *Madam*

I would like to make a ² _____ for a single ³ _____ for three ⁴ _____, 24, 25, and 26 November. I would like a room with a ⁵ _____ of the gardens, if possible. Could you send me some ⁶ _____ about the spa treatments?

⁷ _____ confirm the reservation.

⁸ _____

Sylvie Vartan

c Complete the e-mail with these words.

~~Madam~~	information	Please	nights
reservation	room	Yours	view

d Complete the chart.

	Informal e-mails (to a friend)	Formal e-mails (to a hotel)
Beginning	Hi / Hello / Dear (*Antonio*)	_____ (*Sir / Madam / Mr. Smith*)
End	Hope to hear from you soon. All the best / Love	Please _____ (*the reservation*). _____
Name	First name only	First name and _____

WRITE an e-mail to one of the hotels to make a reservation for you and your partner, family, etc.

Say…
- what room(s) you would like (single, double, how many).
- when you want to go (number of nights and dates).

Ask…
- for a room with a view and information about something.
- the hotel to confirm the reservation.

Check your e-mail for mistakes.

GRAMMAR

Circle the correct sentence, a or b.

(a) Hi. I'm Susanna.
b Hi. I Susanna.

1   a   The Earth is hoter than Mars.
     (b) The Earth is hotter than Mars.

2   (a) Tea is cheaper than coffee.
     b   Tea is more cheap than coffee.

3   a   Driving is dangerouser
       than flying.
     (b) Driving is more dangerous
       than flying.

4   (a) Your English is worse than mine.
     b   Your English is more bad
       than mine.

5   (a) It's the cheapest restaurant in
       the city.
     b   It's the cheaper restaurant in
       the city.

6   a   What's the better time to visit?
     (b) What's the best time to visit?

7   (a) Would you like to do a parachute
       jump?
     b   Do you like to do a parachute
       jump?

8   (a) I'd like to drive a Ferrari.
     b   I'd like drive a Ferrari.

9   (a) You speak very slow.
     b   You speak very slowly.

10   a   She plays tennis very good.
      (b) She plays tennis very well.

10

VOCABULARY

a   adjectives and adverbs

Write the opposite adjective or
adverb.

good   *bad*
1 quickly   *slowly*
2 safe   *unsafe*
3 well   *unwell*
4 noisy   *quiet*
5 the best   *the worst*

b   word groups

Circle the word that is different.

Ireland	(Chinese)	Thailand	Spain
1 careful	tall	serious	generous
2 cold	hot	dry	dangerous
3 bigger	hotter	leader	older
4 friendly	quietly	dangerously	carefully
5 noisy	crowded	expensive	safe

c   prepositions

Complete the sentences with *for*, *in*, *than*, *of*, or *up*.

Look *at* the board.

1 It's the hottest country _____ the world.
2 The best time _____ year to visit is the spring.
3 I bought a present _____ my sister.
4 Would you like to go _____ in a balloon?
5 My brother is taller _____ me.

15

PRONUNCIATION

a   Underline the word with a different sound.

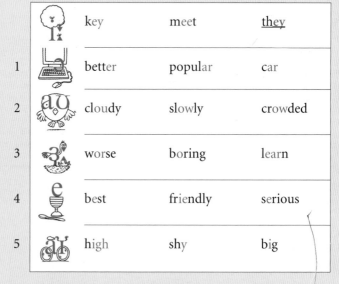

	key	meet	<u>they</u>
1	better	popular	car
2	cloudy	slowly	crowded
3	worse	boring	learn
4	best	friendly	serious
5	high	shy	big

b   Underline the stressed syllable.

infor<u>ma</u>tion

aggressive   ambitious   adventure   politely   dangerously

10

CAN YOU UNDERSTAND THIS TEXT?

a Look at the photo and read the article quickly. Would you like to go there?

b Read the article again. Circle a, b, or c.

1 In the Atacama desert…
   a it hardly ever rains.
   b it never rains.
   c it sometimes rains.

2 The only people who live there are…
   a NASA scientists.
   b villagers.
   c builders.

3 The people in Chungungo…
   a have more water than before.
   b have a lot of water.
   c can't water their plants.

4 The Atacama is a very good place to go if you want to…
   a see clouds.
   b see mountains.
   c see stars.

The Atacama desert…

…the perfect place for people who are looking for adventure

The Atacama desert in Chile is a spectacular place. There is very little vegetation, and it looks like the moon – in fact NASA tested their lunar vehicles here. There are some very big volcanoes. Almost nobody lives there, but there are some small villages on the edge of the desert. Life is hard and everything needs to be imported – food, building materials, and of course water.

In 1971 it rained in the Atacama. People were amazed because the last time it rained there was 400 years earlier, in 1570! It is the driest place in the world. But in the village of Chungungo they are now getting water from the fog clouds which come in from the sea. Daisy Sasmaya, a villager, says, 'We are very happy because now we can have a shower every day, and we can water our plants every week.'

The sky over the Atacama desert is hardly ever cloudy, so it is one of the best places in the world to see the stars. The biggest observatory in the world is being built on top of a mountain. 'It's the purest air in the world,' says journalist Hugh O'Shaughnessy. 'At night the sky is incredibly clear – you feel that there is nothing between you and Mars.'

Adapted from a British magazine

CAN YOU HEAR THE DIFFERENCE?

8.18 Nicolas, a French student at university in Edinburgh, talks about his first impressions. Listen. Circle a or b.

1 In Scotland people speak…
   a with a different accent and some different words.
   b with a different accent only.

2 In Edinburgh…
   a it's very windy but it doesn't rain much.
   b it rains more than in Paris.

3 Nicolas's Scottish friends…
   a eat a lot of fruit and vegetables.
   b eat a lot of sweet things.

4 Nicolas…
   a never drinks whisky.
   b drinks whisky when he goes to the pub.

5 When he finishes university he…
   a is going to go home.
   b doesn't know what he is going to do.

CAN YOU SAY THIS IN ENGLISH?

a Can you…? Yes (✓)

☐ say what the weather is like today (three sentences)
☐ compare your town / city with another (three sentences)
☐ say three superlative sentences about cities in your country (e.g. *The biggest city is…*)
☐ say three things you would like to do (e.g. *go up in a balloon*)
☐ say three different ways that people can drive (e.g. *slowly*)

b Complete the questions.

are	do	does	did	would	is	were	do

1 What _____ you do last weekend?
2 How often _____ you do sport or exercise?
3 Where _____ you like to go next summer?
4 _____ your town have many tourist sights?
5 _____ you like cooking?
6 _____ you going to go out tonight?
7 What _____ the teacher wearing today?
8 Where _____ you at ten o'clock last night?

c Interview your partner. When he / she answers, try to ask another question.

9

A

G present perfect
V *been to*
P sentence stress

Before we met

> Have you been to Madrid?
> No, I haven't. But I've been to Barcelona.

1 SPEAKING & READING

a In pairs, answer the questions.

ARE YOU JEALOUS?

1 Are you jealous?
   - [ ] often
   - [ ] sometimes
   - [✓] hardly ever / never
2 Can you remember a time when you were jealous of…?
   a a brother or sister
   b a friend
   c another person
3 Do you know a very jealous person? Who?
4 Who do you think are more jealous, men or women? *Women*

b **9.1** Read and listen to the beginning of a story and answer questions 1–3.

1 Which cities has Rob visited? Tick (✓) the boxes.

   Barcelona [ ]
   Lisbon [ ]
   Madrid [ ]
   Rome [✓]
   Venice [ ]
   Florence [✓]

2 Who is Jessica? Where is she now?

3 Why doesn't Charlotte want to go to these three places?

c In pairs, guess the meaning of the highlighted words. Check with your teacher or a dictionary.

> **Rob is going out with Charlotte, a woman who works in the same company as him. They want to go away somewhere for the weekend.**

It was a Thursday evening in June when we sat down in Charlotte's living room with the holiday brochures . 'I got these from the travel agent's today,' said Charlotte. 'This is going to be fun ! Have you been to Italy?'

'Yes, I have,' I replied . 'I've been to Rome and Florence.'

'On holiday?'

'Yes… with Jessica.'

'Oh.' There was a long silence .

'But I haven't been to Venice. What about Venice?'

'No. Forget Italy. Have you been to Spain?'

'Yes. I've been to Barcelona.'

'With Jessica?'

'Yes, but…'

She picked up a brochure for Lisbon. 'Don't tell me. You've been there too. With Jessica.'

'No. I've never been to Portugal. Look, what's the problem? Jessica's not my girlfriend now. She's thousands of miles away. She lives in Canada. Why are you so jealous of her?'

'Me? Jealous? I'm not jealous.'

There was another long silence.

2 GRAMMAR present perfect

a Look at this sentence from the story in **1** and answer questions 1–4.

I've been to Rome and Florence.

1 Does Rob know Rome and Florence? **yes / no**
2 Do we know exactly *when* Rob went to Rome and Florence? **yes / no**
3 What verb is *'ve*?
4 What verb is *been*?

b Look at the story in **1** again. <u>Underline</u> ⊞, ⊟, and ? examples of *have been (to)*.

c Complete the chart with *have, has, haven't,* or *hasn't.*

	⊞	⊟	?
I, you, we, they	I _have_ been to Rome.	I _have_ been to Venice.	_have_ you been to Lisbon?
he, she, it	She _has_ been to Rome.	She _has_ been to Venice.	_have_ he been to Lisbon?

has

d ○ **p.138 Grammar Bank 9A.** Read the rules and do the exercises.

3 PRONUNCIATION sentence stress

a **9.2** Listen and repeat this dialogue. <u>Copy</u> the <u>rhy</u>thm.

A <u>Have</u> you <u>been</u> to <u>Italy</u>?
B <u>Yes</u>, I <u>have</u>. I've <u>been</u> to <u>Venice</u>.
A <u>Have</u> you <u>been</u> to New <u>York</u>?
B <u>No</u>, I <u>haven't</u>. I <u>haven't</u> <u>been</u> to the <u>USA</u>.

b Play *Have you been to…?*

4 LISTENING

a **9.3** Listen to the rest of the conversation between Rob and Charlotte. Who phones?

b Listen again. Complete the sentences with *Charlotte, Rob,* or *Jessica.*

1 _____ hasn't been to Paris.
2 _____ likes the hotel.
3 _____'s mobile rings.
4 It is _____.
5 _____ doesn't want to talk on the phone to _____.
6 _____ is angry with _____ and leaves the house.

5 SPEAKING

Stand up and move around the class. Ask *Have you been to…?* questions until somebody answers 'yes'. Write their name in the questionnaire.

Find a person who...

has been to a very hot country	_____
has been to a karaoke bar	_____
has been to a big sports event	_____
has been to an opera	_____
has been to a spa	_____
has been to a fortune teller	_____
has been to another continent	_____
has been to a big pop concert	_____

G present·perfect or past simple?
V past participles
P irregular past participles

Have you seen the film?
Did you like it?

I've read the book, I've seen the film

1 SPEAKING

CINEMA EXPERIENCES

Have you ever...?		Yes	No	
1	*spoken* to a film actor or actress		✓	Who was it? What did you say?
2	seen a film more than three times	✓		What film? When was the last time you saw it?
3	cried in a film		✓	What film was it? Why did you cry?
4	played a 'soundtrack' from a film	✓		What film was it? Did you like the film?
5	leaved the cinema in the middle of a film		✓	What film was it? Why did you leave?
6	slept in the cinema		✓	What film was it? Why did you sleep?
7	somebody in the back row			Who was it? Did you see the film?

a Complete the questionnaire above with these past participles.

slept   bought   cried   kissed   left   ~~spoken~~   seen

b Interview a partner with the questionnaire. If he / she says 'Yes, I have', ask the other two questions.

2 VOCABULARY past participles

a Look at the past participles in 1a. Which ones...?

1 are regular _____ _____
2 are irregular (and the same as the past simple)

_____ _____ _____

3 are irregular (and different from the past simple)

_____ _____ _____

b ➡ **p.154 Irregular verbs.** Highlight the past participles that are different from the past simple.

3 PRONUNCIATION irregular participles

a Put three irregular past participles in each column.

begun	bought	broken	caught	done
driven	drunk	given	known	made
paid	spoken	taken	worn	written

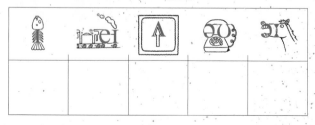

b ▶ 9.4 Listen and check. Practise saying them.

4 GRAMMAR present perfect or past simple?

a Look at the dialogue. In pairs, answer the questions.

1 What tense is question **A**?
2 What tense are questions **B** and **C**?
3 Which question is general?
4 Which questions are specific?

> **A Have you ever spoken to an actor or actress?**
> Yes, (I have).
> **B Who was it?**
> Jude Law.
> **C What did you say to him?**
> I asked him for his autograph.

b ● **p.138 Grammar Bank 9B**. Read the rules and do the exercises.

5 LISTENING & SPEAKING

a Look at the four books and answer the questions.
   • Have you read the book?
   • Have you seen the film(s)?

b Read the website information about *The Book Programme* on Radio South. What is tonight's programme about? What are listeners going to do?

> **The Book Programme – listeners' phone-in.**
>
> **Our question tonight:** Do good books make good films? When a book becomes a bestseller, we know that a film version is soon going to appear. But which is usually better, the book or the film?
>
> **Phone 0845 8769922 and tell us what you think.**

c **9.5** Listen to Carl, Linda, and Sam phoning the programme. Which person is *most* positive about films made from books?

d Listen again. Mark the sentences T (true) or F (false).

1 Carl thinks books are usually better than films.
2 He loved the *Lord of the Rings* films.
3 Linda says people read a lot.
4 She thinks people buy books after they see a film.
5 Sam thinks good books make bad films.
6 He preferred the James Bond books.

e In pairs, think of a film based on a book and make a class list on the board.

f Look at the chart. What are the questions?

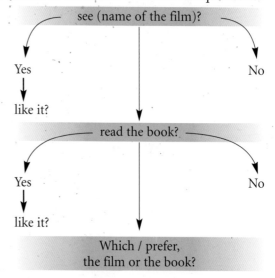

g In pairs, ask and answer about the films in **e**.

FILE 5 Grammar Bank p.130

In pairs or small groups, circle a, b, or c.

1 _____ the first American president?
   a Were he   b Did he be   c Was he
2 They _____ the tickets at a travel agent's.
   a didn't book   b didn't booked   c don't booked
3 I _____ a lot last night.
   a studyed   b studied   c studed
4 **A** What _____ last night?
   B I went out.
   a you did   b did you   c did you do
5 What time _____ to bed?
   a did you went   b did you go   c went you

FILE 6 Grammar Bank p.132

In pairs or small groups, circle a, b, or c.

1 How many bathrooms _____ in the house?
   a is there   b are there   c there are
2 _____ a good film on TV last night.
   a There is   b There was   c There were
3 Listen! The neighbours _____ again!
   a argue   b arguing   c are arguing
4 **A** What _____?
   B They're doctors.
   a are they doing   b do they do   c they do
5 The museum _____ at 9 o'clock.
   a opens   b is opening   c open

FILE 7 Grammar Bank p.134

In pairs or small groups, circle a, b, or c.

1 There isn't _____ milk.
   a some   b an   c any
2 I _____ water.
   a don't drink many   b don't drink much
   c drink quite
3

_____ coffee do you drink?

   a How much   b How many   c How
4 Where _____ to go next summer?
   a do you go   b you going   c are you going
5 I'm sure you _____ very happy.
   a are going to be   b go to be   c are going be

FILE 8 Grammar Bank p.136

In pairs or small groups, circle a, b, or c.

1 Are cars _____ in Britain than in the USA?
   a expensiver   b most expensive
   c more expensive

2 Butter is _____ for you than olive oil.
   a badder   b worse   c worst

3

This is _____ building in the city.

   a the old   b the most old   c the oldest

4 _____ fly a plane?
   a Do you like   b Would you like to
   c You would like

5 Americans drive _____.
   a carefully   b careful   c carefuly

FILE 9 Grammar Bank p.138

In pairs or small groups, circle a, b, or c.

1 _____ Paris or Rome?
   a Have you been   b Have you been to
   c Have you be to

2 I've read the book but I haven't _____ the film.
   a see   b saw   c seen

3 **A** Have you ever met anyone famous?
   B Yes, I _____.
   a have   b do   c did

4 _____ she driven a Ferrari before?
   a Did   b Has   c Do

5 We _____ to Italy last year.
   a go   b have been   c went

Do the exercises in pairs or small groups.

a Circle the word that is different.

	Ireland	(Chinese)	Thailand	Spain
1	France	Brazil	Polish	Spain
2	lawyer	footballer	cooker	teacher
3	grandmother	son	uncle	brother
4	angry	fast	tired	hot
5	usually	often	sometimes	yesterday
6	saw	buy	got	heard
7	sofa	armchair	living room	mirror
8	chemist's	art gallery	supermarket	square
9	carrots	beans	strawberries	potatoes
10	carefully	good	fast	aggressively

b Write the next word.

one, two, *three*

1 thirty, forty, _____
2 Sunday, Monday, _____
3 first, second, _____
4 tenth, twentieth, _____
5 morning, afternoon, _____
6 once, twice, _____
7 second, minute, _____
8 summer, autumn, _____
9 February, March, _____
10 last week, this week, _____

c Answer the questions.

What's the opposite of *big*? *small*

1 What's the sixth month of the year?
2 Who is your mother's sister?
3 In which room do you have a shower?
4 What's the opposite of *clean*?
5 What's the past tense of *think*?
6 Where can you buy stamps and send a letter?
7 What language do they speak in Argentina?
8 Who is the person who serves you in a restaurant?
9 What's the opposite of *love*?
10 What do you call a person who likes giving presents?

d Complete the verbs.

play football

1 g_____ married
2 h_____ breakfast
3 g_____ shopping
4 d_____ housework
5 m_____ a noise
6 t_____ photos
7 t_____ off your mobile phone!
8 g_____ someone a present
9 p_____ the piano
10 w_____ for the bus

e What can you see? Label the pictures.

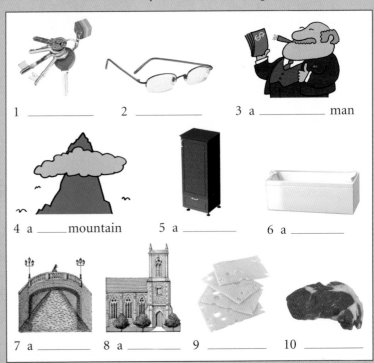

1 _____ 2 _____ 3 a _____ man

4 a _____ mountain 5 a _____ 6 a _____

7 a _____ 8 a _____ 9 _____ 10 _____

f Complete the sentences with a preposition.

1 Marco's Italian. He's _____ Venice.
2 The British often talk _____ the weather.
3 My brother's _____ university. He's studying French.
4 How often do you listen _____ music?
5 What time did you get _____ this morning?
6 There's a TV _____ the bedroom.
7 I drink a lot _____ water.
8 What did you have _____ breakfast?
9 His flat is next _____ mine.
10 Have you ever been _____ Morocco?

Pronunciation

Do the exercises in pairs or small groups.

a <u>Underline</u> the word with a different sound.

	key	meet	<u>they</u>
1	meat	speak	bread
2	garden	glasses	famous
3	work	bought	saw
4	word	first	four
5	three	this	there
6	German	job	get
7	home	love	know
8	how	hour	hairdresser
9	see	sugar	she
10	five	give	mine
11	play	have	make
12	house	daughter	shower
13	what	not	don't
14	cinema	cards	music
15	cooker	footballer	food

b <u>Under</u>line the stressed syllable.

infor<u>ma</u>tion

1 American
2 afternoon
3 thirteen
4 breakfast
5 July
6 musician
7 between
8 bathroom
9 tomorrow
10 pronunciation
11 sunglasses
12 magazine
13 chocolate
14 umbrella
15 receptionist
16 grandmother
17 dangerous
18 museum
19 supermarket
20 newspaper

6B Room 11 **Students A+B**

→ Memory test **A** p.109 **B** p.112

Communication

5A Three Presidents **Student A**

Ask and answer questions with **B** to complete the information about Presidents Washington, Lincoln, and Roosevelt. You start.

What was Washington's first name?

President	Washington	Lincoln	Roosevelt
First name?	_____	Abraham	_____
Which president?	First	_____	26th
born (year)?	_____	1809	_____
born (place)?	Westmoreland, Virginia	_____	New York City, New York
parents from?	Virginia	Virginia	_____

5D Police interview **Student A**

Work in pairs with another **A**. You are police officers. There was a robbery last night. **B** and **B** are two friends. You think they were responsible. They say that they went out for dinner and went to the cinema last night. You want to know if this is true.

a Look at the Police interview form and prepare to ask the **Bs** the questions. Think of more questions to get more details about the evening, e.g. *What did you wear? What did you eat and drink? What film was it?*

b Interview *one* of the **Bs**. Write down his / her answers in the form. (Your partner interviews the other **B**.)

Police interview form

Name: _____ Date: _____

	What time?	Where?	More details
/ meet?			
/ have dinner?			
/ go to the cinema?			
What / do after the cinema?			
What time / get home?			

c Compare with your partner. Did the two **Bs** tell exactly the same story? If not, arrest them!

6B Memory test **Student A**

a Write questions from the prompts.

1 / a cupboard in the room?
   Was there a cupboard in the room?
2 How many tables / ?
3 / a lamp on the table?
4 Where / the TV?
5 What colour / the walls?
6 / any pictures? How many?

b Ask **B** your questions.

c Answer **B**'s questions.
   Who has the best memory?

6C They're having a party! Student A

You and **B** have the same picture but with eight differences.

a Tell **B** what is happening in the **left** side of your picture. **B** will tell you what is different in his / her picture. Circle the differences.

b Listen to **B** telling you what is happening in the **right** side of his / her picture. Look at your picture. Tell **B** the differences. Circle them on your picture.

c When you've finished, compare the two pictures.

8A The True False Show Student A

€10,000   €20,000   €30,000   **€40,000**   €50,000   €60,000   **€70,000**   €80,000

a Complete the sentences with the comparative of the **bold** adjective.

1 **fast**   A horse is _____ than a tiger. (**False**)
2 **expensive** Tokyo is _____ than New York. (**True**)
3 **near**   The Earth is _____ the Sun than Mars is. (**True**)
4 **big**   Africa is _____ than Asia. (**False**)
5 **common**   The letter *i* is _____ than *e* in English. (**False**)
6 **bad**   Black coffee is _____ for you than white coffee. (**False**)
7 **dangerous** Rugby is _____ than skiing. (**True**)
8 **rich**   Switzerland is _____ than Saudi Arabia. (**True**)

b Roleplay *The True False Show*. You are the quiz presenter, **B** is the contestant.
• Read sentence 1 to **B**. **B** says if it's true or false.
• If **B** is right, he / she gets €10,000. Continue with sentence 2, etc.
• If **B** gets the answer wrong, he / she loses everything and starts from the beginning again.

c Change roles. Now **B** is the presenter.

d Who won more money, you or **B**?

Communication

5A Three Presidents **Student B**

Ask and answer questions with **A** to complete the information about Presidents Washington, Lincoln, and Roosevelt. **A** starts.

President	Washington	Lincoln	Roosevelt
First name?	George	_____	Theodore
Which president?	_____	16th	_____
born (year)?	1732	_____	1858
born (place)?	_____	Hodgenville, Kentucky	_____
parents from?	_____	Virginia	New York

5B Sydney

Sydney, Nova Scotia, population 26,000

Raoul and Emma were in Sydney, but not Sydney, Australia. They were in Sydney, Nova Scotia, in north-east Canada!

The story of Emma and Raoul was on television and in newspapers around the world. They stayed in Sydney, Nova Scotia, for four days and then travelled home on Air Canada to London, England (not London, Canada).

5D Police interview **Student B**

> Work in pairs with another **B**. You are friends. Last night you met, had dinner, and went to the cinema. There was a robbery last night. **A** and **A** are police officers. They think you were responsible, and they want to interview you separately. If you both tell the same story, you are innocent.

a Prepare your story. Use these questions. Think of extra details, e.g. *What did you wear? What did you eat and drink? What film was it?*

- What time / where did you meet?
- What time / where did you have dinner?
- What time / where did you go to the cinema?
- What did you do after the cinema?
- What time did you get home?

b Answer **A**'s questions.

c Did you and your friend tell the same story?

6B Memory test **Student B**

a Write questions from the prompts.

1 / a carpet in the room?
   Was there a carpet in the room?
2 How many beds / ?
3 / the door open or closed?
4 What / on the bed?
5 What colour / the curtains?
6 / any books in the room?

b Answer **A**'s questions.

c Ask **A** your questions. Who has the best memory?

6C   They're having a party!   **Student B**

You and **A** have the same picture but with eight differences.

a   Listen to **A** telling you what is happening in the **left** side of his / her picture. Look at your picture. Tell **A** the differences. Circle them on your picture.

b   Tell **A** what is happening in the **right** side of your picture. **A** will tell you what is different in his / her picture. Circle the differences.

c   When you've finished, compare the two pictures.

8A   The True False Show   **Student B**

€10,000   €20,000   €30,000   **€40,000**   €50,000   €60,000   **€70,000**   €80,000

a   Complete the sentences with the comparative of the **bold** adjective.

1 **good**	Red wine is _____ for you than white wine. (**True**)
2 **safe**	Driving is _____ than flying. (**False**)
3 **old**	The Parthenon is _____ than the Pyramids. (**False**)
4 **intelligent**	Dolphins are _____ than chimpanzees. (**True**)
5 **small**	Spain is _____ than Germany. (**False**)
6 **short**	The Second World War was _____ than the First World War. (**False**)
7 **popular**	Basketball is _____ than football. (**True**)
8 **long**	A kilometre is _____ than a mile. (**False**)

b   Roleplay *The True False Show*. **A** is the quiz presenter, you are the contestant. Say if **A**'s sentences are true or false.

c   Change roles. Now you are the presenter.

•   Read sentence 1 to **A**. **A** says if it's true or false.

•   If **A** is right, he / she gets €10,000. Continue with sentence 2, etc.

•   If **A** gets the answer wrong, he / she loses everything and starts from the beginning again.

d   Who won more money, you or **A**?

Listening

5.1

We are now at Mount Rushmore, in South Dakota, and you can see in front of you, from left to right, the heads of George Washington, Thomas Jefferson, Theodore Roosevelt, and Abraham Lincoln. As you know, all four men were Presidents of the United States of America. George Washington was the first president…

5.6

They walked to the information desk and they showed their tickets to the woman.

Raoul When is our next flight?

Woman The next flight? This is the end of your journey. Where did you want to go?

Raoul Where are we?

Woman You're in Sydney.

Raoul We're in Australia?

Woman Australia? No, you're in Canada!

Raoul Canada!

5.11

Interviewer Sílvia, from Rio de Janeiro, went out with four friends, Karina, Mônica, Ana, and Thelma. Sílvia, can you tell us about your girls' night out?

Sílvia Sure.

Interviewer What did you wear?

Sílvia I wore jeans and a jacket – and two friends wore the same!

Interviewer And what did you do?

Sílvia Well, first we went to a restaurant in Ipanema. It's a place where a lot of famous people go and we saw an actor there, called Fernando Pinto. Karina really likes him – in fact she's crazy about him! Then we went to a beach bar and we had some drinks. And then later we went to a party.

Interviewer What did you have to eat and drink?

Sílvia At the restaurant we had beer and we had some French fries. And at the beach bar we had beer and coconut water.

Interviewer What did you talk about?

Sílvia About men, of course! What else?

Interviewer How did you go home?

Sílvia By taxi. I have a car, but I don't like driving at night.

Interviewer What time did you get home?

Sílvia Very, very late – I don't remember exactly what time.

Interviewer So, did you have a good time?

Sílvia Yes, it was good. Not fantastic, but good – seven out of ten!

5.17

Then the inspector questioned Barbara Travers.

Inspector What did you do after dinner yesterday evening?

Barbara After dinner? I played cards with Gordon, and then I went to bed.

Inspector What time was that?

Barbara It was about half past eleven. I remember I looked at my watch.

Inspector Did you hear anything in your father's room?

Barbara No. I didn't hear anything.

Inspector Did you have any problems with your father?

Barbara No, no problems at all. My father was a wonderful man and a perfect father.

Inspector Thank you, Miss Travers.

5.18

Next the inspector questioned Gordon Smith.

Inspector What did you do after dinner, Gordon?

Gordon I played cards with Barbara. Then she went to bed.

Inspector Did you go to bed then?

Gordon No. I stayed in the sitting room and I had a glass of whisky. Then I went to bed.

Inspector What time was that?

Gordon I don't remember exactly. I didn't look at the time.

Inspector Did you hear anything during the night?

Gordon No, I didn't. I was very tired. I slept very well.

Inspector You and Mr Travers were business partners, weren't you?

Gordon Yes, that's right.

Inspector And it's a very good business I understand.

Gordon Yes, inspector, it is.

Inspector And now it is *your* business.

Gordon Listen, inspector, I did not kill Jeremy. He was my partner and he was my friend.

5.19

Finally the inspector questioned Claudia Simeone.

Inspector What did you do yesterday evening, after dinner?

Claudia I went to my room and I had a bath and I went to bed.

Inspector What time was that?

Claudia About 11.00.

Inspector Did you hear anything?

Claudia Yes. I heard somebody go into Jeremy's room. It was about 12.00.

Inspector Who was it?

Claudia It was Amanda, his wife.

Inspector Are you sure? Did you see her?

Claudia Well no, I didn't see her. But I'm sure it was Amanda.

Inspector You were Mr Travers' secretary, Claudia.

Claudia Yes, I was.

Inspector Were you *just* his secretary?

Claudia What do you mean?

Inspector Were you in love with Mr Travers?

Claudia No, I wasn't.

Inspector The truth please, Claudia.

Claudia Very well, inspector. Yes, I was in love with him and he said he was in love with me. He said he wanted to leave his wife – Amanda – and marry me. I was stupid. I believed him. He used me, inspector! I was very angry with him.

Inspector Did you kill him?

Claudia No, inspector, I loved Jeremy.

Before dinner, Gordon had a drink with Jeremy in the library.

Gordon Cheers, Jeremy. Happy birthday.

Jeremy Ah, thanks, Gordon.

Gordon Listen, Jeremy, I want to talk to you about Barbara.

Jeremy Barbara? What's the problem?

Gordon It's not exactly a problem. I am in love with her, and I want to marry her.

Jeremy Marry Barbara? Marry my daughter! Are you crazy? Never. You don't love Barbara. You only want her money!

Gordon That's not true, Jeremy. I love her.

Jeremy Listen to me. If you marry Barbara, when I die all my money goes to Claudia.

Gordon To Claudia? To your secretary?

Jeremy Yes.

Gordon Is that your last word, Jeremy?

Jeremy Yes, it is.

Amanda Dinner everybody!

At midnight Gordon finished his whisky and went upstairs.

Jeremy Who is it? Gordon?

Mark Hi, Allie. Wow! You look great. Nice dress!

Allie Oh, thank you. Er, this is for you – for your birthday. I bought you a little present. Oh! Oh no. I hope it's not broken.

Mark It's a mug! It *was* a mug. Thanks, Allie!

Allie I don't believe it! I'm sorry, Mark.

Mark No problem. It was really nice of you.

Allie I'll get you another one tomorrow.

Mark Don't worry. Listen, did you call a taxi to go to the restaurant?

Allie No, I have my car outside. Come on, it's time to go. I booked the table for 8.00 and I'm not sure exactly where the restaurant is.

Mark Hey, Allie, relax. This isn't work. This is a night out.

Allie Sorry. I'm a bit stressed today. OK. Let's go.

Estate agent OK. Let's have a look upstairs now. Follow me.

Louise It's very old.

Estate agent Yes, madam, the house is a hundred years old. The Travers family lived here for nearly eighty years. There are five bedrooms. This was Mr Travers' bedroom.

Larry It's cold in here.

Louise Yes, very cold.

Estate agent Don't worry, madam. There is central heating in the house. And this room here is the second bedroom.

Larry OK, well what do you think, Louise?

Louise I like it.

Larry Me too. Yup. We want it.

Estate agent Excellent! Let's go back to my office and we can sign the contract.

Larry Good evening.

Barman Good evening, sir, madam. What would you like to drink?

Larry Do you have champagne?

Barman Yes, sir.

Larry A bottle of champagne, please.

Barman Here you are!

Louise Cheers, Larry.

Larry Cheers. To our new house.

Barman You're Americans, aren't you?

Louise Yes, that's right. We're from Washington.

Larry My wife and I just rented the big house in the village. Tonight is our first night there.

Barman The Travers family's old house?

Larry Yes.

Barman Oh.

Louise Is there a problem?

Barman Didn't they tell you?

Larry Tell us what?

Barman About the murder.

Louise Murder??

Barman Yes, Mr Travers was murdered in that house in 1938… in his bed.

Louise Oh, how horrible!

Barman That's why they always rent that house.

Larry Why?

Barman Because nobody wants to buy it.

Louise Come on, Larry. Let's go and find a hotel.

Larry A hotel?

Louise Yes – I don't want to sleep in a house where somebody was murdered. Come on.

Larry Louise… your champagne… Louise…

Stephen In the middle of the night I suddenly woke up! It was 2.00. The television was off! But how? There was no remote control, and I certainly didn't get up and turn it off. The light was still on, but suddenly the light went off too. Now I was really frightened! I couldn't see anything strange, but I could feel that there was somebody or something in the room. I got out of bed and turned on the TV again. Little by little I started to relax, and I went to sleep again. When I woke up it was morning. I had breakfast and I left the hotel about 10.00.

Interviewer So the question is, did you see the ghost?

Stephen No, I didn't see the ghost, but I definitely felt something or somebody in the room when I woke up in the night.

Interviewer Were you frightened?

Stephen Yes, I was! Very frightened!

Interviewer Would you like to spend another night in the hotel?

Stephen Definitely, yes.

Interviewer Why?

Stephen Well, I'm sure there was something strange in that room. I can't explain the television and the light. I want to go back because I want to see the ghost.

Listening

6.12

Hi Bill, it's Rob. What are you doing?… I'm going to London… Who are you talking to?… I'm having a coffee… Is the baby crying?… My train's arriving. Bye!

6.14

1 I'm from Edinburgh.
2 He's from London.
3 They live in Brighton.
4 We went to Oxford for the weekend.
5 She was born in Dublin.
6 We're studying in Cambridge.
7 I want to go to Manchester.
8 Do you like Birmingham?

6.18

Allie OK. It's this street. No, it isn't. I'm sure she said the first on the right.
Mark No, she said the *second* on the right. Relax, Allie.
Allie Look, let's ask that man there.
Mark I don't think he knows. He's a tourist.
Allie Just ask him, please.
Mark OK, OK. Excuse me! We're lost. Do you know where King Street is?
Man Sorry, I don't live here – I'm a tourist.
Mark You see. I was right.
Allie OK, let's try the second on the right.
Mark Here it is. King Street. I *knew* she said the second on the right.
Allie There's the restaurant, Donatella's. Can you see anywhere to park?
Mark That white car's going over there! Do you think you can park in that space?
Allie Are you saying I can't park?
Mark Allie, I'm only joking.
Allie OK, OK, I'm sorry.

7.2

Bob Good evening. My name's Bob, and welcome to another edition of … *Can men cook?*
Audience Yes, they can!
Bob Well, Belinda, who's our first guest tonight?
Belinda This is Colin Davidson and he's from Bristol!
Bob Hello, Colin! What can you cook?
Colin Hello, Bob. My speciality is spaghetti bolognese.
Bob And what do you need to make it, Colin?
Colin Well, for four people you need some spaghetti. About half a kilo, Bob. And then for the bolognese sauce you need an onion, some butter, a carrot, some mushrooms, some tomato ketchup…
Bob Tomato *ketchup*, Colin?
Colin Yes, that's right, and you also need some red wine.
Bob Do you need any meat, Colin?
Colin Yes, Bob. You need some meat – about 300 grams. And some cheese.

Bob What kind of cheese?
Colin Any kind. It doesn't matter.
Bob OK. So those are all the ingredients. The question now is – *Can men cook?*
Audience Yes, they can!
Bob Colin, you have exactly 30 minutes to make us… spaghetti bolognese!
Colin Well, Bob, first you cut up the onion and you fry it. Then you take the…
Bob OK, Colin. That's your thirty minutes. And now it's time to taste the spaghetti bolognese. And it looks… mm, delicious. Belinda, can you try it for us? Well, Belinda, what do you think of it? Can men cook?
Belinda Mmm. Yes, Colin, it's er very interesting. I'm sure your wife loves your cooking.
Colin I'm not married, Belinda. Would you like to have dinner with me?
Bob Well, that's all we have time for. Until *next* week. It's goodbye from me Bob Keen, Belinda Leyton, and Colin Davidson from Bristol.

7.6

Jerry Hello?
Peter Hello! Is that Jerry Harte?
Jerry Speaking.
Peter This is Peter Douglas from the programme *Changing Holidays*.
Jerry Oh, hello!
Peter Is your holiday planned for next week, Jerry?
Jerry Yes, it is.
Peter Where are you going to go?
Jerry We're going to go to Norway.
Peter Who are you going to go with?
Jerry With Sue, my girlfriend.
Peter How are you going to get there?
Jerry By train.
Peter What are you going to do there?
Jerry We're going to clean a river and plant some trees. It's a working holiday!
Peter Oh, very interesting. Where are you going to stay?
Jerry We're going to stay at a campsite.
Peter Well, Jerry, you're not going to go camping, because you're not going to go to Norway. We're going to *change your holiday*!
Jerry Oh, so where are we going to go?

7.8

Peter Well, here we are at the airport with Lisa and Jon and Jerry and Sue. And this is the moment of truth. I've got two envelopes here, and now I'm going to give the two couples their *new* holiday plans! Are you ready to play 'Changing Holidays'?
All Yes.
Peter OK, so now you can open the envelopes. Jon and Lisa first.
Jon A working holiday in Norway.
Lisa Oh no!

Peter Oh yes! You're going to help clean a river and plant some trees.

Jon Oh great. Working all day!

Lisa Where are we going to stay?

Peter You're going to stay at a campsite!

Lisa A campsite? Oh no, I hate camping!

Peter And now Sue and Jerry.

Sue Oh! A week in New York.

Jerry New York?

Peter That's right. You're going to spend a week in the Big Apple, shopping, going out, and seeing the sights! Do you like shopping, Jerry?

Jerry Not much.

Sue What are we going to wear? We don't have the right clothes for New York.

7.9

Peter OK, so it's hello again to our two couples from last week, Lisa and Jon, and Sue and Jerry. Welcome back. So what we all want to know is, did you have a good time? Jon and Lisa, what about you?

Jon No, we didn't have a good time. It wasn't a holiday. I mean, we worked every day.

Lisa And it was hard work. That's not my idea of a holiday.

Jon And we hated camping!

Lisa The people were very nice but…

Jon It rained every day. We went to bed at 10.00 every night – not exactly exciting!

Lisa The thing is, what we really like is shopping, nightlife, big cities – and if that's what you want, Norway's not the place to go.

Peter OK, OK. What about Sue and Jerry. Did *you* have a good time?

Sue Well, we don't usually like big cities. But New York is special!

Jerry Yeah. The hotel wasn't very good – it was very big and impersonal. But we liked all the tourist sights – the Guggenheim was fantastic.

Sue And the people were great, and we loved the food.

Jerry Yeah, we even liked the nightclub! We usually go to bed early, we're not really 'night' people, but the New York nightlife is great.

Peter So where are you going to go next summer? Lisa and Jon?

Lisa Next summer we're really going to go to New York!

Peter And Jerry and Sue?

Sue We really liked New York. Next year we're going to go to another city, maybe Amsterdam or Barcelona!

7.19

Mark How was the pasta?

Allie It was delicious.

Mark Listen, Allie. There's something I want to ask you.

Allie Yes? What?

Waiter Would you like a dessert?

Allie Yes, please. What is there?

Waiter Tiramisu, ice cream, or fruit salad.

Allie Fruit salad, please.

Waiter And you, sir?

Mark Nothing for me, thanks. Allie?

Allie Yes. Go on, Mark.

Mark Well, tomorrow's my last day. And I think we… I mean, I really liked meeting you and…

Waiter Here you are. Fruit salad. Would you like any coffee?

Allie Yes, an espresso, please.

Mark The same for me, please.

Allie Sorry, Mark.

Mark Do you want to come to California next month? There's a big conference. I'm going to be there. Why don't you come? What do you think?

Waiter Two espressos. Anything else? A little brandy? A grappa?

Mark No, thank you. What do you say, Allie?

Allie I'm not sure, Mark. I need some time to think about it, OK?

Mark All right. But please tell me before I go.

Allie OK.

Mark Could we have the check, please?

Waiter Sorry? The check?

Allie The bill, Mark. We're in Britain, remember?

Mark Sorry. Could we have the bill, please?

Waiter Yes, sir.

8.1

Presenter Good evening. Welcome to *The True False Show*. Tonight's show comes from Dublin. My name's Annie O'Brian and I ask the questions. Remember, after each question you have ten seconds to say 'true' or 'false'. If you get the first answer right, you win 10,000 euros. If you get the second answer right, you win 20,000 euros, and you win 30,000 euros for the third correct answer. For eight correct answers you win 80,000 euros. But if you get an answer wrong, you go home with … nothing. Our first contestant is Darren from London. Right, Darren, for 10,000 euros. Mosquitoes are more dangerous than sharks. True or false?

Darren Er, true.

Presenter Correct. Mosquitoes are more dangerous than sharks. More people die every year from mosquito bites than from shark attacks. Now, for 20,000 euros, brown eggs are healthier than white eggs. True or false?

Darren Er… false.

Presenter Correct. It's false. Brown eggs *look* nicer than white ones, but they are exactly the same. For 30,000 euros, the Earth is hotter than Mars.

Darren I think it's true, Annie.

Presenter Correct. The Earth is much hotter than Mars. Next, for 40,000 euros, coffee is more popular than tea in the UK. True or false?

Darren Er, false.

Presenter Correct. British people drink 185 million cups of tea every day. Next, for 50,000 euros, tigers are better swimmers than cats. True or false?

Darren Er… false. No – true.

Presenter Is that your answer?

Darren Yes, true.

Presenter Correct. Tigers are very good swimmers. For 60,000 euros, an adult is shorter in the morning than in the evening.

Darren Er… false.

Listening

Presenter Correct. Adults are one centimetre *taller* in the morning than in the evening. OK Darren, for 70,000 euros. White cars are safer than yellow cars. True or false?

Darren Er, I'm sure that's false, Annie.

Presenter Correct. Yellow cars are safer – they are easier to see during the day, so they don't have as many accidents.
And finally, the last question. Be very careful, Darren. If you get it right, you win 80,000 euros, but if you get it wrong, you lose everything. Are you ready?

Darren Yes, ready.

Presenter OK, so for 80,000 euros. The word 'yes' is more common than the word 'no'. True or false?

Darren Er… er…

Presenter Quickly Darren, time's running out.

Darren True.

Presenter No, Darren. It's false. 'No' is more common than 'yes'. You *had* 70,000 euros, but now you go home with *nothing*.

8.4

Presenter Hello again. Today we talk to Dr Alan Baker, a psychologist, about car colour and personality. Good evening, Dr Baker.

Dr Baker Good evening!

Presenter So, what does the colour of our cars say about our personality?

Dr Baker Well, let's start with yellow. People who drive yellow cars are usually very friendly. This colour is more popular with women than with men.

Presenter And white?

Dr Baker A white car shows that you are careful. It's the favourite colour car for doctors – they buy more white cars than any other colour.

Presenter What about other colours?

Dr Baker Well, let's take red. People who choose red cars are usually more aggressive drivers than normal. With blue cars, it's the opposite. If you have a blue car it means you are probably quiet.

Presenter What about green?

Dr Baker People with green cars are usually generous.

Presenter And what about black?

Dr Baker Well, people who like black cars are usually serious people. Business people often choose black cars.

Presenter We've got time for one more colour. What about silver?

Dr Baker Yes, well if you have a silver car it means you are stylish.

Presenter Er, what colour is your car, Dr Baker? White?

Dr Baker No, it's red, actually.

Presenter Thank you very much, Dr Baker. And now we turn our attention…

8.11

Interviewer Russell, can you describe your day?

Russell Well, first we had some classes and we learned how to land.

Interviewer What happened then?

Russell Well, when we finished the classes we went up in the plane.

Interviewer How high did you go up?

Russell About 800 metres.

Interviewer Then what happened?

Russell Well, I sat on the floor and waited.

Interviewer How did you feel?

Russell Very frightened! That was the worst part, waiting to jump.

Interviewer And then?

Russell Then the instructor said 'Jump!' and I jumped.

Interviewer How was it?

Russell It was incredible. First I fell very fast. I couldn't think. I forgot all the instructions. Suddenly the parachute opened, and I floated down.

Interviewer Did you land OK?

Russell Yes, I did – perfectly.

Interviewer How did you feel afterwards?

Russell Great – I felt fantastic. I was really happy. I thought 'I did it!'

Interviewer Would you like to do it again?

Russell Well no, I wouldn't.

Interviewer Why not?

Russell Because it can be dangerous. One of the people in my group broke his leg. And two months after that I heard that someone died.

Interviewer How?

Russell His parachute didn't open and he fell…

8.17

Mark Hello?

Allie Hi, Mark, it's Allie. I'm really sorry but the traffic this morning is terrible. I'm going to be very late.

Mark OK.

Allie I think the best thing is for you to take a taxi to the station and then get the train to the airport.

Mark No problem, I'll call a taxi. Well, thanks for everything…

Allie No listen, I'll meet you at the airport – we can say goodbye there.

Mark All right. Where can we meet?

Allie At the information desk.

Mark OK, see you there.

Allie Bye.

Mark Excuse me, change of plan. Could you call me a taxi, please? To the station.

Hello. Sorry I can't take your call. Please leave a message after the tone.

Mark Hi, Allie, this is Mark. Where are you? I'm at the information desk. My flight leaves in forty minutes.

Allie Mark! Mark! Sorry I'm late!

Mark Don't worry – I'm just happy you got here.

Allie Come on. You're going to miss your flight.

Mark Wait a minute. Are you going to come to the conference in California? Am I going to see you again?

Allie The plane's going to leave without you.

Mark Allie?

Allie I asked my boss this morning, and he said yes. I can go!

Mark Great! Oh, I don't have your home phone number.

Allie Don't worry. I'll e-mail it to you tomorrow.

This is the final call for all passengers on flight BA287 to San Francisco. Please proceed immediately to Gate 12.

Mark Goodbye, Allie. And thanks for everything.

Allie Goodbye, Mark. Have a safe trip!

Mark See you in California. Bye.

9.3

Rob Why don't we go to Paris? I haven't been there.

Charlotte Are you sure?

Rob Look, I promise. I've never been to Paris.

Charlotte OK. Let's look at the brochure.
I love Paris. It's one of my favourite cities.

Rob You choose a hotel then.

Charlotte What about this one? It's very near the Eiffel Tower.
It looks nice. Very romantic. Let's go there.

Rob Is that your phone?

Charlotte No, it's yours.

Rob Oh yeah. You're right. Hello?… Who?… Oh hi. What a surprise… Fine, fine. How are you?… Sorry?… It's seven o'clock here. In the evening. What time is it in Canada?… Sorry?… No, I'm not. I'm with… I'm with a friend… Can I call you back later?… I said, can I call you back later this evening?… Sorry? I can't hear you… OK I'll call you back later… Yes, OK. Bye… Sorry, Charlotte, what did you say about the hotel?

Charlotte Forget it, Rob. I don't want to go away with you this weekend. In fact I don't want to do anything with you. See you sometime.

Rob Charlotte, don't go. Listen, I can explain. It isn't what you think…

9.5

Presenter Our next caller is Carl from Essex. Hello, Carl.

Carl Hi.

Presenter What do you think, Carl? Do good books make good films?

Carl Well, I've read a lot of books and then seen the films, and I usually think that the books are better. For example, I loved the *Lord of the Rings* books but I didn't like the films very much.

Presenter Thank you, Carl. Our next caller is Linda from Manchester. Hello, Linda.

Linda Hi. Well, what I think is that today people don't read very much. But they do go to the cinema. And sometimes *after* they've seen a film of a book then they go and buy the book, so that's a good thing because they read more.

Presenter But do you think good books make good films?

Linda Yes. I've read a lot of good books and then I've seen the films and I've loved them all, *The Exorcist, Harry Potter, Gone with the Wind.* They're all great books and great films.

Presenter Thank you, Linda. And our last caller is Sam from Cardiff. Hello, Sam. What do you think about our question today?

Sam I think it depends. I think good books *don't* usually make good films. But I've seen some films which I think are *better* than the books. That's usually because the book *wasn't* very good.

Presenter So bad books can make good films?

Sam That's right.

Presenter Give me an example.

Sam Well, the James Bond films. The books aren't very good but some of the films are great, like *Goldfinger*, or *From Russia with Love*.

Presenter Thank you, Sam. Bye.

5A past simple of *be*: *was / were*

+				−			
I	**was**			I	**wasn't**		
You	were			You	weren't		
He / She / It	**was**	famous.		He / She / It	**wasn't**	famous.	
We	were			We	weren't		
You	were			You	weren't		
They	were			They	weren't		

?				✔			✘	
Was	I			I **was**.			I **wasn't**.	
Were	you			you **were**.			you **weren't**.	
Was	he / she / it	famous?	Yes,	he / she / it **was**.	No,		he / she / it **wasn't**.	
Were	we			we **were**.			we **weren't**.	
Were	you			you **were**.			you **weren't**.	
Were	they			they **were**.			they **weren't**.	

- **Contractions**: *wasn't = was not, weren't = were not.*
- Use *was / were* to talk about the past.
  *My grandfather **was** born in London.*

5B past simple regular verbs

+			−	
I			I	
You			You	
He / She / It	**worked**		He / She / It	**didn't work**
We	yesterday.		We	yesterday.
You			You	
They			They	

spelling rules for regular verbs

Infinitive	Past	Spelling
watch play	watch**ed** play**ed**	add -*ed*
live smoke	live**d** smoke**d**	add -*d*
stop	stop**ped**	one vowel + one consonant = double consonant
study	stud**ied**	consonant + *y* > *ied*

?			✔			✘		
	I			I			I	
	you			you			you	
Did	he / she / it	**work**		he / she / it	**did**.	No,	he / she / it	**didn't**.
	we	yesterday?	Yes,	we			we	
	you			you			you	
	they			they			they	

- **Contraction**: *didn't = did not.*
- Use the past simple for finished actions.
- Regular verbs in the past + end in -*ed*,
  e.g. *worked, lived, played.*
- The past is the same for all persons.
- Use *did / didn't* + infinitive for
  past ? and −.

5C past simple irregular verbs

Infinitive	Past +	Past −
go	went	didn't go
have	had	didn't have
get	got	didn't get
buy	bought	didn't buy
leave	left	didn't leave
drive	drove	didn't drive
meet	met	didn't meet
see	saw	didn't see
wear	wore	didn't wear
do	did	didn't do

- Use the irregular past form only in + sentences.
  *I **saw** a film last night.*
- Use the infinitive after *did / didn't.*
  ***Did** you **see** a film last night?* NOT ~~Did you saw…?~~
- Remember word order = **ASI** (auxiliary, subject, infinitive)
  or **QUASI** (question word, auxiliary, subject, infinitive).
  Did you go out last night?
  Where did you go?

> ⚠ Past of *can = could.*
> − = *couldn't* NOT ~~didn't can~~
> ? = *Could you…?* NOT ~~Did you can…?~~

5A

a Change the sentences from present to past.

Present simple	Past simple
I'm tired.	I _was_ tired last week.
1 Today is Sunday.	Yesterday _____ Saturday.
2 Where are you now?	Where _____ you yesterday?
3 We are in Munich today.	We _____ in Berlin yesterday.
4 I'm in Italy this month.	I _____ in France last month.
5 My father's a pilot.	My grandfather _____ a pilot too.
6 It isn't open now.	It _____ open this morning.
7 Why aren't you at work today?	Why _____ you at work yesterday?

b Complete the dialogues with *was, wasn't, were,* or *weren't.*

A _Were_ you and Susan at the party last night?
B Yes, we 1 _____.
A 2 _____ it good?
B No, it 3 _____. The music 4 _____ awful. Where 5 _____ you?
A I 6 _____ ill.

A Where 7 _____ you born?
B I 8 _____ born in Australia in 1919.
A 9 _____ your parents Australian?
B No, they 10 _____. My mother 11 _____ Italian and my father 12 _____ Greek.

5B

a Rewrite the sentences in the past simple with *yesterday.*

Present	Past
I use the Internet.	_I used the Internet yesterday._
1 I watch TV.	_____
2 Do you listen to the radio?	_____
3 We study English.	_____
4 He doesn't work.	_____
5 The film finishes at 7.00.	_____
6 I don't like the film.	_____
7 Does she smoke?	_____
8 They play tennis.	_____

b Complete the sentences with a verb in the past simple.

arrive   not book   land   live   stay
not remember   turn on   want   watch

I _turned on_ the TV.
1 We _____ in a three-star hotel last year.
2 They _____ a table and the restaurant was full.
3 _____ you _____ the football on TV last night?
4 Sorry. I _____ it was your birthday yesterday.
5 I _____ with my parents when I was a student.
6 Why _____ you _____ to be a doctor?
7 He _____ late for work and the boss was angry.
8 When the plane _____ she _____ her mobile phone.

5C

a Complete the text with the verbs in brackets in the past simple.

Yesterday _was_ my birthday. (be)
My boyfriend 1 _____ me a beautiful jacket. (buy)
In the evening we 2 _____ out. (go)
I 3 _____ my new jacket. (wear)
We 4 _____ for a Chinese restaurant (look)
but we 5 _____ find one, (not can)
so we 6 _____ dinner in our favourite Italian restaurant. (have)
After that we 7 _____ a film. (see)
Then we 8 _____ two friends at a nightclub. (meet)
We 9 _____ for two hours. (dance)
We 10 _____ home until 3.00. (not get)
I 11 _____ very tired, (be)
and I 12 _____ straight to bed. (go)

b Complete the questions in the past simple.

Did you go out last night? (you / go out)
1 What _____? (you / wear)
2 Where _____? (you / go)
3 What _____? (you / do)
4 _____ with you? (your sister / go)
5 What _____ to eat? (you / have)
6 What time _____? (the party / finish)
7 What time _____? (you / get home)
8 _____ a good time? (you / have)

6

6A *there is / there are*

	Singular	Plural
+	**There's** a piano.	**There are** some glasses in the cupboard.
−	**There isn't** a fridge.	**There aren't** any pictures.
?	**Is there** a TV?	**Are there** any glasses?
✔ ✘	Yes, **there is**. No, **there isn't**.	Yes, **there are**. No, **there aren't**.

- We often use *there is / are* with *a / an*, *some*, and *any*.
- Use *some* and *any* with plural nouns. *Some* = not an exact number.
- Use *some* in + sentences and *any* in − and ?.

⚠ Be careful. *There is* and *It is* are different.
There's *a key on the table.* **It's** *the key to the kitchen.*

6B *there was / there were*

	Singular	Plural
+	**There was** an old TV.	**There were** only three guests.
−	**There wasn't** a remote control.	**There weren't** any more people.
?	**Was there** a ghost?	**Were there** any lights?
✔ ✘	Yes, **there was**. No, **there wasn't**.	Yes, **there were**. No, **there weren't**.

- *there was / were* is the past of *there is / are*.

6C present continuous: *be* + verb + *-ing*

+

Full form	Contraction	
I **am**	I**'m**	
You **are**	You**'re**	crying.
He / She / It **is**	He / She / It**'s**	**having** a party.
We **are**	We**'re**	**arguing**.
You **are**	You**'re**	
They **are**	They**'re**	

−

Full form	Contraction	
I **am not**	I**'m not**	
You **are not**	You **aren't**	crying.
He / She / It **is not**	He / She / It **isn't**	**having** a party.
We **are not**	We **aren't**	**arguing**.
You **are not**	You **aren't**	
They **are not**	They **aren't**	

?   **✘**

?		✔		✘	
Am I			I **am**.		I**'m not**.
Are you			you **are**.		you **aren't**.
Is he / she / it	crying?	Yes,	he / she /it **is**.	No,	he / she / it **isn't**.
Are we	**having** a party?		we **are**.		we **aren't**.
Are you	**arguing?**		you **are**.		you **aren't**.
Are they			they **are**.		they **aren't**.

- Use the present continuous for things that are happening now.
  It's raining. *The baby's crying.*
- For the spelling of the *-ing* form see Grammar Bank 4B.

6D present simple or present continuous?

Present simple	Present continuous
My sister **works** in a bank.	Today she**'s working** at home.
What **do you** usually **wear** to work?	What **are you wearing** now?

- Use the present simple to say what you usually do.
- Use the present continuous to say what you are doing now.

⚠ Be careful with *do*.
   A *What* **do you do**? (= *What's your job?*)
   B *I'm a teacher.*
   A *What* **are you doing**? (= *now, at the moment*)
   B *I'm waiting for a friend.*

6A

a Complete the sentences with *There's* or *There are*.

There's   a sofa in the living room.
1 _____ four cups in the cupboard.
2 _____ a clock in the kitchen.
3 _____ lots of chairs.
4 _____ a garage.
5 _____ some pictures on the wall.
6 _____ a desk in the study.

b Write +, −, or ? sentences with *there is / are*.

  + chairs / the garden   *There are some chairs in the garden.*
1 + table / the kitchen
2 ? fireplace / the living room
3 − plants / the living room
4 ? cupboards / the kitchen
5 − shower / bathroom
6 + shelves / study

6B

a Look at the hotel information. Write a + or − sentence with *There was / were*.

Hotel Astoria	
single rooms	✗
double rooms	✓
swimming pool	✓
restaurant	✓
car park	✗
shops	✗

There weren't any single rooms.
1 _____
2 _____
3 _____
4 _____
5 _____

b Complete with the correct form of *there was* or *there were*.

A How many guests *were there* in the hotel?
B 1 _____ _____ four including me. 2 _____ _____ a French tourist and 3 _____ _____ two businessmen.
A 4 _____ _____ a restaurant?
B No, 5 _____ _____, but 6 _____ _____ a bar.
A What 7 _____ _____ in your room?
B 8 _____ _____ a minibar and a TV.
A 9 _____ _____ two beds?
B No, 10 _____ _____. 11 _____ _____ a double bed.

6C

a Write a question and answer for each picture.

1 *What's he doing?*   He _____.
2 _____ ?   _____.
3 _____ ?   _____.

b Put the verbs in brackets in the present continuous.

A Hello.
B Oh, hi Dad. Where are you?
A I'm in my hotel. *I'm having* a drink in the bar. (have) It 1 _____ a lot here. Is Mum there? (rain)
B Yes, but she 2 _____ to somebody on the mobile just now. (talk)
A Oh. What 3 _____ you _____? (do)
B My friend Matt is here.
A Matt? Why 4 _____ you _____ your homework? (not do)
B Don't worry. We 5 _____ together. (study)
A Where's Jenny?
B She 6 _____ for Kevin to come. (wait) They 7 _____ a party tonight. (have)
A Oh. What 8 _____ she _____? (wear)
B Nothing special. OK Dad, here's Mum. Bye.

6D

a Right or wrong? Tick (✓) or cross (✗) the sentences.

It rains at the moment. ✗
1 Listen! The baby's crying. ☐
2 My neighbours often argue. ☐
3 John's on holiday. He has a great time. ☐
4 My brother's staying with us at the moment. ☐
5 I'm normally going to the gym after work. ☐
6 **A** Where are you going?   **B** To the shops. ☐
7 **A** What are you doing?   **B** I'm a teacher. ☐

b Put the verbs in brackets in the present simple or continuous.

Where *are* you *going*? (go)   To play football – see you later!
1 **A** Hi, Sarah! What _____ you _____ here? (do)
   B I _____ for my boyfriend. (wait)
2 **A** What _____ your mother _____? (do)
   B She's a nurse. She _____ at the local hospital. (work)
3 Listen! They _____ a party upstairs again. (have) They _____ a party at least once a month! (have)
4 I _____ to the supermarket. (go) _____ you _____ anything? (want)

7

7A countable / uncountable nouns

- There are two kinds of noun in English, countable (C) and uncountable (U).
  C = things you can count. C nouns can be singular or plural.
  one apple, two apples, **three** apples.
  U = things you can't count. U nouns can't be plural.
  butter, meat NOT ~~two butters, three meats~~
- Some nouns can be C or U but the meaning is different.

an ice cream → / ← some ice cream

a / an, some / any

		Countable	Uncountable
⊞	We need	**an** apple. **some** apples.	**some** butter. **some** milk.
⊟	We don't need	**a** tomato. **any** tomatoes.	**any** rice. **any** sugar.
?	Do we need	**a** tomato? **any** tomatoes?	**any** rice? **any** sugar?

- Use *a / an* with singular C nouns.
- Use *some* with plural C nouns and U nouns in ⊞.
- Use *any* with plural C nouns and U nouns in ⊟ and ?.

⚠ We can also use *some* in ? to ask for and offer things.
Can I have **some** *coffee?*
Would you like **some** *biscuits?*

7B how much / how many?

Uncountable (singular)	Full answers	Short answers
How much water do you drink?	I drink **a lot of** water. I drink **quite a lot of** water. I don't drink **much** water. I don't drink **any** water.	▌A lot. Quite a lot. Not much. None.
Countable (plural)		
How many sweets did you eat?	I ate **a lot of** sweets. I ate **quite a lot of** sweets. I didn't eat **many** sweets. I didn't eat **any** sweets.	▌A lot. Quite a lot. Not many. None.

- Use *How much...?* with uncountable (U) nouns and *How many...?* with plural countable (C) nouns.
- Use: *a lot (of)* with C and U nouns for a **big quantity**.
  quite a lot (of) for **quite a big quantity**.
  not...much with U nouns for a **small quantity**.
  not...many with C plural nouns for a **small quantity**.
  not...any (*none* in short answers) for **zero quantity**.

7C be going to (plans)

⊞

Full form	Contraction	
I **am** You **are** He / She / It **is** We **are** You **are** They **are**	I**'m** You**'re** He / She / It**'s** We**'re** You**'re** They**'re**	**going to have** a holiday next month.

⊟

Full form	Contraction	
I **am not** You **are not** He / She / It **is not** We **are not** You **are not** They **are not**	I**'m not** You **aren't** He / She / It **isn't** We **aren't** You **aren't** They **aren't**	**going to have** a holiday next month.

? / ✔ / ✘

			✔		✘	
Am I **Are** you **Is** he / she / it **Are** we **Are** you **Are** they	**going to have** a holiday next month?	Yes,	I **am**. you **are**. he / she /it **is**. we **are**. you **are**. they **are**.	No,	I'm **not**. you **aren't**. he / she / it **isn't**. we **aren't**. you **aren't**. they **aren't**.

- Use *be going to* + verb (infinitive) to talk about future plans.
- With the verb *go* you can say *I'm going to go* OR *I'm going ~~to go~~*.
- We often use future time expressions with *going to*.
  tomorrow, next week, next year, etc.

⚠ *next year* NOT ~~the next year~~

7D be going to (predictions)

You can also use *be going to* + verb (infinitive) for predictions.

(I think) They're going to be very happy.

(I think) It's going to rain.

7A

a Write *a*, *an*, or *some* + a food / drink word.

1 _some cereal_   6 _____
2 _____   7 _____
3 _____   8 _____
4 _____   9 _____
5 _____   10 _____

b Complete the dialogue with *a*, *an*, *some*, or *any*.

A I invited my sister for dinner. Is that OK?
B No, it isn't. We don't have _any_ food!
A There are ¹ _____ eggs and ² _____ cheese. I can make ³ _____ omelette.
B There aren't ⁴ _____ eggs. I had the last two.
A We can make ⁵ _____ pasta. Are there ⁶ _____ tomatoes?
B Yes. And there's ⁷ _____ onion. What about drink? Is there ⁸ _____ wine?
A Yes, there's ⁹ _____ bottle of red wine. And there's ¹⁰ _____ Coke too.

7B

a Complete with *How much* / *How many*.

How much fruit do you eat?

1 _____ people were there at the party?
2 _____ milk does she drink?
3 _____ coffee did you drink yesterday?
4 _____ eggs are there in the fridge?
5 _____ cents are there in a euro?
6 _____ money do you have with you?
7 _____ hours does your baby usually sleep?
8 _____ free time do you have during the week?

b ~~Cross out~~ the wrong words.

I don't eat ~~much~~ / **many** apples.

1 I eat **a lot of** / **much** fruit.
2 Do you drink **much** / **many** water?
3 We don't buy **much** / **many** vegetables.
4 **A** How much meat do you eat?
   B **None** / **Any**. I'm a vegetarian.
5 I eat **quite a lot of** / **quite** fish.
6 **A** How much exercise do you do?
   B **No much** / **Not much**.

7C

a Write sentences about Susan's holiday plans.

She's going to go to Rome. (go)
1 _____ Italian. (speak)
2 _____ a hotel. (stay in)
3 _____ photos. (take)
4 _____ spaghetti. (eat)
5 _____ Colosseum. (see)

b Complete the sentences with (*be*) *going to* + a verb.

buy   cook   do   not have   study   not fly

Our car is ten years old. We _'re going to buy_ a new one.
1 My mother's at work so my father _____ the lunch.
2 I _____ tonight. I have an exam tomorrow.
3 _____ you _____ a present for Bill?
4 We _____ to Edinburgh. It's too expensive.
5 What _____ your brother _____ after school?
6 It's her birthday next week, but she _____ a party.

7D

a Write predictions for the pictures.

1 *It's going to* _____
2 _____
3 _____
4 _____

b Complete the predictions with (*be*) *going to* and a verb.

be   break   have   not pass   wake up   win

It's my dream holiday! I know I _'m going to have_ a good time.
1 They're playing very well. I think they _____ the match.
2 She's a very bad student. She _____ the exam.
3 Look at the blue sky. It _____ a beautiful day.
4 You're driving very fast! We _____ an accident!
5 Be careful with that glass! You _____ it!
6 The baby's very tired. I don't think she _____ tonight.

8A comparative adjectives

White cars are **safer than** yellow cars.
Mosquitoes are **more dangerous than** sharks.
Tigers are **better** swimmers **than** cats.

- Use comparative adjectives + *than* to compare two people / things.

Adjective	Comparative	
old cheap	old**er** cheap**er**	one-syllable adjectives: add *-er*
big hot	big**ger** hot**ter**	adjectives ending one vowel + one consonant: double consonant, add *-er*
healthy happy	health**ier** happ**ier**	one- or two-syllable adjectives ending consonant + *y* > *-ier*
famous expensive	**more** famous **more** expensive	two- or more syllable adjectives: *more* + adjective
good bad far	**better** **worse** **further**	irregular

8B superlative adjectives

It's **the hottest** country in the world.
The most dangerous time is the spring.

- Use *the* + superlative adjective to say which is the (*biggest*, etc.) in a group.

Adjective	Comparative	Superlative	
cold high	cold**er** high**er**	**the** cold**est** **the** high**est**	add *-est*
hot big	hot**ter** big**ger**	**the** hot**test** **the** big**gest**	double consonant, add *-est*
pretty sunny	prett**ier** sunn**ier**	**the** prett**iest** **the** sunn**iest**	> *-iest*
dangerous	**more** dangerous	**the most** dangerous	*the most* + adjective
good bad far	**better** **worse** **further**	**the best** **the worst** **the furthest**	irregular

8C *would like to*

+		−	
I You He She We They	**'d like to** fly a plane.	I You He She We They	**wouldn't like to** fly a plane.

?			✔		✘	
Would	I you he she we they	**like to** fly a plane?	Yes,	I you he she we they	**would.**	No,	I you he she we they	**wouldn't.**

- **Contractions:** *'d = would, wouldn't = would not.*
- *I would like to = I want to* (now or in the future).
- Use the infinitive with *to* after *would like.*
  *I **would like to** learn.* NOT *I would like learn.*
- You can also use *Would you like to…?* for invitations.
  Would you like to *have dinner with me tonight?*

⚠ *Would like* and *like* are different.
  I'd like *to dance.* (= I want to dance now or in the future)
  I like *dancing.* (= I enjoy it, I like it in general)

8D adverbs

I drive **slowly**.
They speak very **quietly**.
People dress very **well**.

- Use adverbs to say *how* people do things.
- Adverbs usually go after the verb.
  I speak English very well.
  NOT *I speak very well English.*
- Look at the chart for how to make adverbs.

Adjective	Adverb	
slow quick bad careful	slow**ly** quick**ly** bad**ly** careful**ly**	+ *-ly*
healthy easy	health**ily** eas**ily**	consonant + *y* > *-ily*
good fast hard	**well** **fast** **hard**	irregular

- Remember the difference between adjectives and adverbs.
  *I'm a **careful** driver.* (adjective)
  *I drive **carefully**.* (adverb)

⚠ Not all words that end in *-ly* are adverbs, e.g. *friendly* = adjective.
  *He's a **friendly** person.*

8A

a Write the comparative form of these adjectives.

hot   _hotter_

1 short   _____
2 difficult   _____
3 beautiful   _____
4 noisy   _____
5 thin   _____
6 near   _____
7 easy   _____
8 rich   _____

b Write comparative sentences.

The Nile / the Amazon (long)
The Nile is longer than the Amazon.

1 Canada / Brazil (big)
2 Tessa / Deborah (pretty)
3 Driving / flying (dangerous)
4 My English / your English (bad)
5 This chair / that chair (comfortable)
6 Her husband / her (young)
7 Buses / trains (cheap)
8 French wine / English wine (good)

8B

a Write the opposite superlative adjectives.

the hottest   _the coldest_

1 the biggest   _____
2 the lowest   _____
3 the cheapest   _____
4 the youngest   _____
5 the easiest   _____
6 the wettest   _____
7 the ugliest   _____
8 the richest   _____

b Complete the sentences with a superlative. Use the adjectives in brackets.

It's _the most dangerous_ country in the world. (dangerous)

1 I am _____ in my family. (tall)
2 That house is _____ in the street. (old)
3 The Scots make _____ whisky in the world. (good)
4 This is _____ part of the country. (hot)
5 This is _____ building in the city. (famous)
6 He's _____ student in the class. (bad)
7 Chinese is one of _____ languages to learn. (difficult)
8 It's _____ dress in the shop. (pretty)

8C

a Write sentences and questions with _would like_.

I / go to New York
I'd like to go to New York.

1 I / be a millionaire.
2 you / be famous?
3 I / not / go up in a balloon
4 he / learn to cook
5 she / not / be on TV
6 they / have children?
7 I / not / live in a foreign country
8 We / like / buy a bigger flat

b Complete these sentences with a verb in the correct form (infinitive or -_ing_).

| be | get | open | cook | go (x 2) | see | live | have | fly | learn |

I'd like _to learn_ to fly a plane.

1 Would you like _____ dinner with me tonight?
2 I'd like _____ to Australia but I don't like _____.
3 She wouldn't like _____ a teacher. She hates children.
4 Do you like _____ wild animals? Would you like _____ on a safari?
5 We'd like _____ married in June.
6 I would like _____ a restaurant because I like _____.
7 Does your sister like _____ in Paris?
8 Would you like _____ another language?

8D

a Adjective or adverb? ~~Cross out~~ the wrong word.

He's very **polite** / ~~politely~~.

1 Our teacher speaks very **slow** / **slowly**.
2 Her German is **perfect** / **perfectly**.
3 Everything happened very **quick** / **quickly**.
4 The food was very **good** / **well**.
5 Please drive **careful** / **carefully**.
6 You can walk **safe** / **safely** at night in this city.
7 My sister dresses very **good** / **well**.
8 The weather is **terrible** / **terribly** tonight.

b Complete the sentences with adverbs from these adjectives.

| bad | ~~good~~ | careful | hard | easy | healthy | slow | quiet | beautiful |

I don't speak French very _well_.

1 We played _____ in the semi-final and we lost 5–1.
2 Hurry up! You're walking very _____.
3 Can you talk _____, please? Your father is asleep.
4 We had a good map and we found their house _____.
5 The boss likes him because he works _____.
6 Open the bag _____. There are eggs inside.
7 He eats very _____ – lots of fruit and vegetables.
8 She sings _____. I'm sure she's going to be famous.

9A present perfect: verb *be*

+

Full form	Contraction	
I **have**	I**'ve**	
You **have**	You**'ve**	
He / She / It **has**	He / She / It**'s**	**been** to Rome.
We **have**	We**'ve**	
You **have**	You**'ve**	
They **have**	They**'ve**	

–

Full form	Contraction	
I **have not**	I **haven't**	
You **have not**	You **haven't**	
He / She / It **has not**	He / She / It **hasn't**	**been** to Venice.
We **have not**	We **haven't**	
You **have not**	You **haven't**	
They **have not**	They **haven't**	

?

			✔		✘	
Have I			I **have**.		I **haven't**.	
Have you			you **have**.		you **haven't**.	
Has he / she / it	**been** to	Yes,	he / she / it **has**.	No,	he / she / it **hasn't**.	
Have we	Paris?		we **have**.		we **haven't**.	
Have you			you **have**.		you **haven't**.	
Have they			they **have**.		they **haven't**.	

- Use the present perfect for general past experiences.
- To make the present perfect use *have / has* + past participle.
- *'s* = *has* in present perfect (but can also be *is* or possessive *'s*).

> ⚠ Compare the present perfect of *be* and the present perfect of *go*.
> *He's **been** to Italy.* = He visited Italy and came back.
> *He's **gone** to Italy.* = He's in Italy now.

9B present perfect: regular and irregular verbs

	Infinitive	Present perfect
Regular verbs	cry	**have cried**
	kiss	**have kissed**
	queue	**have queued**
Irregular verbs	buy	**have bought**
	leave	**have left**
	see	**have seen**
	speak	**have spoken**

- For regular verbs the past participle is the same as the past simple (+ -ed).
- For irregular verbs the past participle is sometimes the same as the past simple, e.g. *buy, bought, bought,* and sometimes different, e.g. *see, saw, seen.*

present perfect or past simple?

Have you seen the film?	Yes, **I have.**
When **did you see** it?	I **saw** it last week.

- Use the present perfect to talk / ask about a general experience in the past.
- Use the past simple to talk / ask about a specific moment in the past.
  *I saw the film **last week**.*
- Don't use the present perfect with *when* and past time expressions, e.g. *yesterday, last week.*
  When did you see it? NOT ~~When have you seen it?~~
  *I **saw** it **last week**.* NOT ~~I've seen it last week.~~

APPENDIX

1 *have got*

+

Full form	Contraction	
I **have got**	I**'ve got**	
You **have got**	You**'ve got**	
He / She / It **has got**	He**'s** / She**'s** / It**'s got**	a car.
We **have got**	We**'ve got**	
You **have got**	You**'ve got**	
They **have got**	They**'ve got**	

–

Full form	Contraction	
I **have not got**	I **haven't got**	
You **have not got**	You **haven't got**	
He / She / It **has not got**	He / She / It **hasn't got**	a car.
We **have not got**	We **haven't got**	
You **have not got**	You **haven't got**	
They **have not got**	They **haven't got**	

?

			✔		✘	
Have I **got**			I **have**.		I **haven't**.	
Have you **got**			you **have**.		you **haven't**.	
Has he / she / it **got**			he / she /it **has**.		he / she / it **hasn't**.	
Have we **got**	a car?	Yes,	we **have**.	No,	we **haven't**.	
Have you **got**			you **have**.		you **haven't**.	
Have they **got**			they **have**.		they **haven't**.	

- You can use *have got* instead of *have* for possession.
  I've got a bike. = I **have** a bike.
  Have you got a car? = **Do you have** a car?
- *have got* is more common in the UK, *have* is more common in the USA and in international English.

9A

a Write the sentences with contractions.

> I have been to Brazil. *I've been to Brazil.*

1 She has not been to the USA.
2 They have not been to China.
3 He has been to an opera.
4 You have not been to my house.
5 I have not been there.
6 We have been to Madrid.

b Write ⊞, ⊟, and ? sentences with *been*.

> ⊞ She / Italy *She's been to Italy.*

1 ⊟ I / Rome
2 ? you / Barcelona
3 ⊟ Mark / South America
4 ⊞ My parents / Africa
5 ? Ann / Argentina
6 ⊟ We / Budapest

9B

a Complete the sentences with the past participles of the verbs in brackets.

> Have you _seen_ my car keys? (see)

1 Have you _____ his new girlfriend? I don't like her. (meet)
2 I've _____ *War and Peace* three times. (read)
3 Have you ever _____ in love? (fall)
4 I've never _____ in the cinema. (cry)
5 My wife has _____ all over the world. (travel)
6 He's _____ a lot of famous people in his work. (meet)
7 She's _____ George Clooney's new film four times. (see)
8 I've _____ a lot of poems but I never show them to anybody. (write)

b Put the verbs in brackets in the present perfect or past simple.

A _Have you ever been_ to the opera? (be)
B Yes, I _went_ last year. (go)
A ¹_____ you ever _____ to a famous actor or actress? (speak)
B Yes, I ²_____ .
A Who ³_____ it? (be)
B Jeremy Irons.
A Where ⁴_____ you _____ him? (see)
B I ⁵_____ him at an airport. (see)
A What ⁶_____ you _____ to him? (say)
B I ⁷_____ him for his autograph. (ask)

A ⁸_____ your brother_____ to South Korea? (be)
B Yes, he ⁹_____ . He ¹⁰_____ to Seoul. (be)
A When ¹¹_____ he _____ there? (go)
B He ¹²_____ there in 2002, to see the World Cup. (go)
A ¹³_____ he _____ it? (like)
B Yes, he ¹⁴_____ it. (love)

Study Link **MultiROM** www.oup.com/elt/englishfile/elementary

2 *will* (future)

⊞		⊟		?			✔			✘		
I You He She It We They	'll write.	I You He She It We They	won't write.	Will	I you he she it we they	write?	Yes,	I you he she it we they	will.	No,	I you he she it we they	won't.

- **Contractions:** *'ll* = *will*, *won't* = *will not*.
- Use *will* + infinitive for:

instant decisions	**I'll call** a taxi.
offers	**I'll help** you.
promises	**I'll e-mail** you tomorrow.

Go, have, get

a Match the verbs and pictures.

- _____ a<u>way</u> (*for the weekend*)
- _____ by bus
- _____ for a walk
- _____ home (*by bus / car*)
- _____ out (*on Friday night*)
- _1_ <u>shopping</u>
- _____ to a <u>restaurant</u> /'restrɒnt/
- _____ to bed (*late*)
- _____ to church / to mosque /mɒsk/
- _____ to the beach

- _15_ <u>break</u>fast / lunch / <u>din</u>ner
- _____ a car
- _____ a drink
- _____ a good time
- _____ a <u>sand</u>wich
- _____ a <u>show</u>er

- _____ a <u>news</u>paper (= buy)
- _____ a <u>taxi</u> / bus / train (= take)
- _____ an <u>e</u>-mail / letter (= receive)
- _____ dressed
- _____ home (= a<u>rrive</u>)
- _____ to a <u>res</u>taurant (= arrive)
- _23_ up

b What's the difference between *go home* and *get home*?

c Cover the expressions and look at the pictures. Test yourself or a partner.

⊙ **p.56**

1 Rooms

Match the words and pictures.

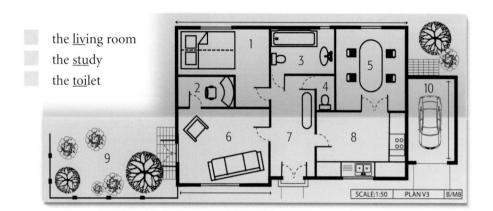

3   the <u>bath</u>room /ˈbɑːθruːm/

1   the <u>bed</u>room

    the <u>din</u>ing room /ˈdaɪnɪŋ/

    the <u>gar</u>age /ˈgærɑːʒ/

    the <u>gar</u>den

    the hall /hɔːl/

8   the <u>kit</u>chen /ˈkɪtʃɪn/

    the <u>liv</u>ing room

    the <u>stud</u>y

    the <u>toi</u>let

2 Furniture and decoration

a Match the words and pictures.

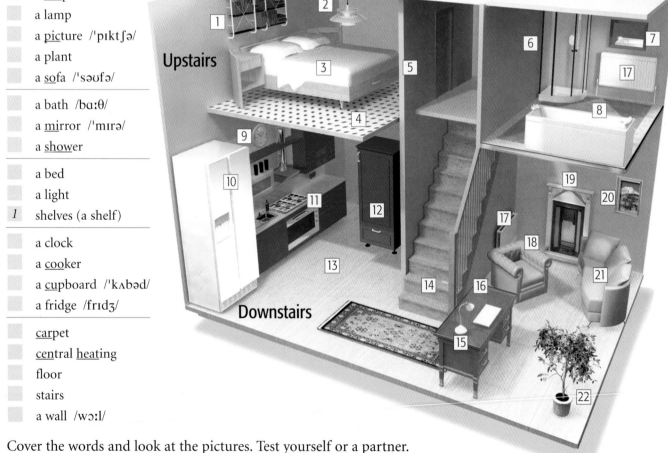

    an <u>arm</u>chair

    a desk

    a <u>fire</u>place

    a lamp

    a <u>pic</u>ture /ˈpɪktʃə/

    a plant

    a <u>so</u>fa /ˈsəʊfə/

    a bath /bɑːθ/

    a <u>mir</u>ror /ˈmɪrə/

    a <u>show</u>er

    a bed

    a light

1   shelves (a shelf)

    a clock

    a <u>cook</u>er

    a <u>cup</u>board /ˈkʌbəd/

    a fridge /frɪdʒ/

    <u>car</u>pet

    <u>cen</u>tral <u>heat</u>ing

    floor

    stairs

    a wall /wɔːl/

b Cover the words and look at the pictures. Test yourself or a partner.

c What things do you have in your house / flat?

🔾 **p.64**

a Match the words and pictures.

an <u>art</u> gallery

a <u>castle</u> /ˈkɑːsl/

a <u>cinema</u> /ˈsɪnəmə/

a mu<u>seum</u> /mjuˌziəm/

a <u>theatre</u> /ˈθɪətə/

a bank

a <u>chemist's</u> / <u>pharmacy</u> /ˈkemɪsts/

a de<u>part</u>ment store

a <u>market</u>

a <u>shopping</u> <u>centre</u> /ˈsentə/

a <u>supermarket</u>

a <u>bridge</u> /brɪdʒ/

a park

a <u>river</u> /ˈrɪvə/

a road

a <u>square</u> /skweə/

a street

a <u>bus</u> station

a <u>railway</u> <u>station</u>

a <u>travel</u> <u>agent's</u>

a church

a mosque

a <u>hospital</u>

1 a po<u>lice</u> <u>station</u>

a <u>post</u> office

a school

a <u>sports</u> <u>centre</u>

a town <u>hall</u>

b Cover the words and look at the pictures.
Test yourself or a partner.

🔾 **p.71**

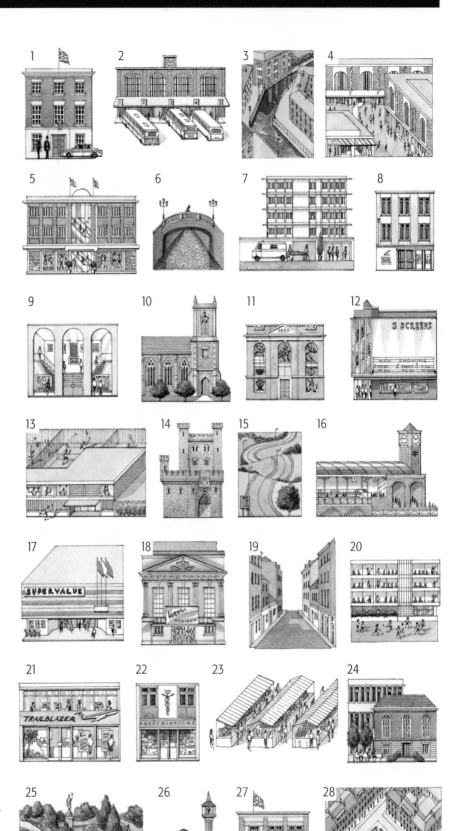

a Match the words and pictures.

Breakfast

Lunch/dinner

Desserts/snacks

Breakfast

	bread /bred/
8	butter
	cereal /ˈsɪəriəl/
	cheese
2	coffee
12	eggs
	jam /dʒæm/
	(orange) juice /dʒuːs/
	milk
6	sugar /ˈʃʊɡə/
	tea
	toast

Lunch / dinner

	fish
	ketchup
23	meat (steak and chicken)
	(olive) oil
	pasta
19	rice
	a salad /ˈsæləd/

Vegetables /ˈvedʒtəblz/

	carrots /ˈkærəts/
	chips (French fries)
	a lettuce /ˈletɪs/
	mushrooms
	an onion /ˈʌnjən/
	peas /piːz/
	potatoes /pəˈteɪtəʊz/
21	tomatoes /təˈmɑːtəʊz/

Desserts / snacks /dɪˈzɜːts/

37	biscuits /ˈbɪskɪts/
	cake
	chocolate /ˈtʃɒklət/
	crisps
	fruit salad
	ice cream
	sandwiches
	sweets

Fruit /fruːt/

29	apples
28	bananas
	grapes
	oranges
	a pineapple

b Cover the words and look at the pictures. Test yourself or a partner.

⊙ p.76

Irregular verbs

PRESENT	PAST SIMPLE	PAST PARTICIPLE
He **is** in Rome. (**be**)	was	been
They **are** in Rome. (**be**)	were	been
The film **begins** at 7.00.	began	begun
She **breaks** his heart.	broke	broken
They **bring** the papers.	brought /brɔːt/	brought
We **build** roads.	built /bɪlt/	built
I **buy** the bread.	bought /bɔːt/	bought
I **can** swim.	could /kʊd/	—
They **catch** the bus.	caught /kɔːt/	caught
She **comes** with her sister.	came	come
It **costs** a lot.	cost	cost
I **do** the housework.	did	done /dʌn/
They **drink** a lot of beer.	drank	drunk
He **drives** a Rolls.	drove	driven
I **eat** a lot.	ate	eaten
She **falls** in love.	fell	fallen
I **feel** angry.	felt	felt
He **finds** a job.	found	found
We **fly** with British Airways.	flew /fluː/	flown /fləʊn/
I **forget** things.	forgot	forgotten
I **get** e-mails.	got	got
He **gives** her presents.	gave	given
They **go** away every weekend.	went	gone /gɒn/
I **have** a car.	had	had
He **hears** a noise.	heard /hɜːd/	heard
I **know** him well.	knew /njuː/	known /nəʊn/

PRESENT	PAST SIMPLE	PAST PARTICIPLE
The train **leave**s at 9.00.	left	left
I **lose** my keys.	lost	lost
We **make** mistakes.	made	made
They **meet** famous people.	met	met
I **pay** the phone bill.	paid	paid
I **put** my car in the garage.	put /pʊt/	put
She **read**s *Time* magazine.	read /red/	read /red/
I **ring** him every day.	rang	rung
He **run**s marathons.	ran	run
He **say**s hello.	said /sed/	said
I **see** my friends every day.	saw /sɔː/	seen
She **send**s a lot of e-mails.	sent	sent
He **sing**s very well.	sang	sung
They **sit** on the sofa.	sat	sat
I **sleep** for eight hours.	slept	slept
We **speak** French.	spoke	spoken
You **spend** a lot on clothes.	spent	spent
She **stand**s up.	stood /stʊd/	stood
I **swim** every day.	swam	swum
I **take** the dog for a walk.	took /tʊk/	taken
They **tell** lies.	told	told
She **think**s of an idea.	thought /θɔːt/	thought
They **throw** tomatoes.	threw /θruː/	thrown /θrəʊn/
I **wake up** in the night.	woke	woken
He **wear**s a hat.	wore	worn
I **win** competitions.	won /wʌn/	won
She **write**s to him.	wrote	written

Vowel sounds

short vowels
long vowels
diphthongs

1 fish /fɪʃ/
2 tree /triː/
3 cat /kæt/
4 car /kɑː/
5 clock /klɒk/
6 horse /hɔːs/
7 bull /bʊl/
8 boot /buːt/
9 computer /kəmpˈjuːtə/
10 bird /bɜːd/
11 egg /eg/
12 up /ʌp/
13 train /treɪn/
14 phone /fəʊn/
15 bike /baɪk/
16 owl /aʊl/
17 boy /bɔɪ/
18 ear /ɪə/
19 chair /tʃeə/
20 tourist /ˈtʊərɪst/

Study Link **MultiROM** www.oup.com/elt/englishfile/elementary

Sounds and spelling

	usual spelling	⚠ but also
fish	**i** his this film six big swim	English women busy
tree	**ee** meet three **ea** speak eat **e** me we	people police key niece
cat	**a** thanks flat black Japan have stamp	
car	**ar** garden party start **a** father glasses dance	aunt
clock	**o** hot stop coffee long not box	what watch want
horse	**or** sport door **al** talk small **aw** saw draw	water four bought thought
bull	**u** full put **oo** good book look room	could would woman
boot	**oo** school food **u*** June use **ew** new flew	do fruit juice shoe
bird	**er** her verb **ir** first third **ur** nurse turn	learn work world word
computer	Many different spellings. /ə/ is always unstressed. <u>tea</u>cher <u>u</u>mbrella <u>A</u>merica fam<u>ou</u>s <u>se</u>cond ag<u>o</u>	

* especially before consonant + **e**

	usual spelling	⚠ but also
egg	**e** yes help ten pet very red	friend bread breakfast any said
up	**u** bus lunch ugly run lucky cut	come brother son does young
train	**a*** name make **ai** rain paint **ay** play day	break steak great eight they grey
phone	**o*** home drove old don't **oa** road toast	slow low
bike	**i*** nine twice **y** my why **igh** high night	buy
owl	**ou** out thousand house count **ow** how brown	
boy	**oi** coin noise toilet **oy** toy enjoy	
ear	**eer** beer engineer **ere** here we're **ear** year hear	really idea
chair	**air** airport stairs fair hair **are** square careful	their there wear
tourist	A very unusual sound. euro Europe poor sure plural	
/i/	A sound between /ɪ/ and /iː/. Consonant + **y** at the end of words is pronounced /i/. happy any thirsty	
/u/	An unusual sound. education usually situation	

Consonant sounds

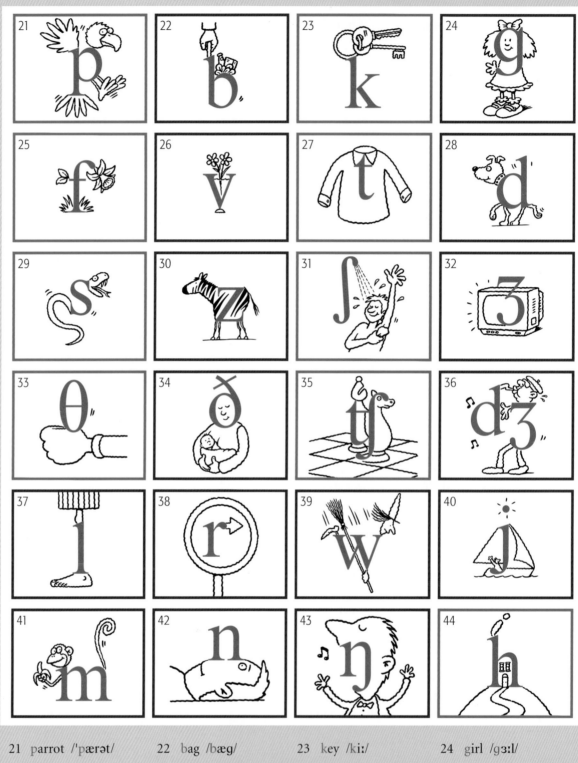

voiced
unvoiced

21 parrot /ˈpærət/   22 bag /bæg/   23 key /kiː/   24 girl /gɜːl/

25 flower /ˈflaʊə/   26 vase /vɑːz/   27 tie /taɪ/   28 dog /dɒg/

29 snake /sneɪk/   30 zebra /ˈzebrə/   31 shower /ˈʃaʊə/   32 television /ˈtelɪvɪʒn/

33 thumb /θʌm/   34 mother /ˈmʌðə/   35 chess /tʃes/   36 jazz /dʒæz/

37 leg /leg/   38 right /raɪt/   39 witch /wɪtʃ/   40 yacht /jɒt/

41 monkey /ˈmʌŋki/   42 nose /nəʊz/   43 singer /ˈsɪŋə/   44 house /haʊs/

Study Link **MultiROM** www.oup.com/elt/englishfile/elementary

Sounds and spelling

		usual spelling	⚠ but also
parrot	**p** **pp**	paper pilot Poland sleep apple happy	
bag	**b** **bb**	be table job builder number rubber	
key	**c** **k** **ck**	credit card actor kitchen like black pick	Christmas chemist's
girl	**g** **gg**	green get angry big eggs bigger	
flower	**f** **ph** **ff**	Friday fifteen wife photo elephant office coffee	
vase	**v**	very eleven live travel river love	of
tie	**t** **tt**	tea take student sit letter bottle	liked dressed
dog	**d** **dd**	dance understand bad read address middle	played tired
snake	**s** **ss**	sister starts smoke stress actress	nice city cinema police
zebra	**z** **s**	zero Brazil music please dogs watches	
shower	**sh** **ti**	shopping shoes Spanish fish station information (+ vowel)	sugar sure
television		An unusual sound. revision decision confusion usually garage	

		usual spelling	⚠ but also
thumb	**th**	think thirty throw bathroom fourth tenth	
mother	**th**	the these then other that with	
chess	**ch** **tch** **t (+ure)**	cheap children church watch match picture adventure	
jazz	**j** **dge**	January juice July enjoy bridge fridge	German manager
leg	**l** **ll**	like little plane girl small spelling	
right	**r** **rr**	red rich problem try sorry terrible	write wrong
witch	**w** **wh**	window twenty Wednesday win why when	one once
yacht	**y** **before u**	yellow yesterday young yes use university	
monkey	**m** **mm**	man Monday money swim summer swimming	
nose	**n** **nn**	no never nine ran dinner thinner	know
singer	**ng**	song England language thing long going	think bank
house	**h**	happy hungry hotel behind hall head	who whose

159

My life is a simple thing that would interest nobody. It is a known fact that I was born, and that is all that is necessary.

Albert Einstein, German scientist

1 GRAMMAR *was / were*

a Complete the sentences with *was, were, wasn't,* or *weren't.*

A Who's that?

B It's William Shakespeare.

A Why ¹___was___ he famous?

B He ²_____ a writer.

A ³_____ he Scottish?

B No, he ⁴_____. He ⁵_____ English. He ⁶_____ born in Stratford-upon-Avon.

A And ⁷_____ he married?

B Yes, he ⁸_____. His wife's name ⁹_____ Anne.

A And ¹⁰_____ they happy?

B I don't know.

b Write questions and answers.

1 Mozart / from / Germany? ✗

Was Mozart from Germany?

No, he wasn't.

2 Columbus and Magellan / explorers? ✓

Were Columbus and Magellan explorers?

Yes, they were.

3 Virginia Woolf / writer? ✓

_____?

_____.

4 the Bee Gees / from the USA? ✗

_____?

_____.

5 John McEnroe / footballer? ✗

_____?

_____.

6 Matisse / composer? ✗

_____?

_____.

7 Picasso / born / Spain? ✓

_____?

_____.

8 Greta Garbo / actress? ✓

_____?

_____.

9 Tolstoy and Cervantes / painters? ✗

_____?

_____.

10 Nelson Mandela / born / Britain? ✗

_____?

_____.

c Complete with present or past forms of *be.*

1 Today __is__ Monday, so yesterday __was__ Sunday.

2 **A** Hi. _____ your sister at home?

B No, she _____. She _____ here this morning, but now she _____ at work.

3 My books _____ here on my desk this morning. Where _____ they now?

4 James _____ born in England, but his parents _____ born in Singapore.

5 My boss _____ angry today because I _____ very late for work yesterday, and this morning too.

Study Link **Student's Book p.130** *Grammar Bank 5A*

2 VOCABULARY word formation

a Make nouns from these words.

1 invent   _an inventor_

2 write   _____

3 politics   _____

4 compose   _____

5 music   _____

6 paint   _____

7 lead   _____

8 act   _____

9 science   _____

10 sail   _____

b Under<u>line</u> the stressed syllables, e.g. _an in<u>ven</u>tor._

c Practise saying the words in **a**.

d Complete the sentences with _was / were_ and a noun from **a**.

1 Galileo _____ _was a scientist_ _____ .

2 The Wright brothers ____ _were inventors_ ____ .

3 Rembrandt _____ .

4 Gustav Mahler _____ .

5 Jimi Hendrix _____ .

6 The Brontë sisters _____ .

7 Gandhi _____ .

8 Nelson _____ .

9 Gregory Peck and Clark Gable _____ .

More Words to Learn

Write translations and try to remember the words.

Word	Pronunciation	Translation
world _noun_	/wɜːld/	
<u>sta</u>tue _noun_	/ˈstætʃuː/	
<u>sol</u>dier _noun_	/ˈsəʊldʒə/	
war _noun_	/wɔː/	
<u>bat</u>tle _noun_	/ˈbætl/	
<u>vill</u>age _noun_	/ˈvɪlɪdʒ/	
great (= important) _adjective_	/ɡreɪt/	
al<u>rea</u>dy _adverb_	/ɔːlˈredi/	
a<u>gainst</u> _preposition_	/əˈɡenst/	
(on the) <u>left</u> (_opposite_ right)	/left/	

Study idea

Try to remember words with other words or phrases:

1 remember words with their opposites, e.g. _left / right_

2 remember words in phrases, e.g. _on the left_

QUESTION TIME ?

Can you answer these questions?

1 Where were you born?

2 Where were your parents born?

3 Were you at home at 6 o'clock yesterday?

4 Who were you with?

5 How old were you on your last birthday?

Study Link MultiROM

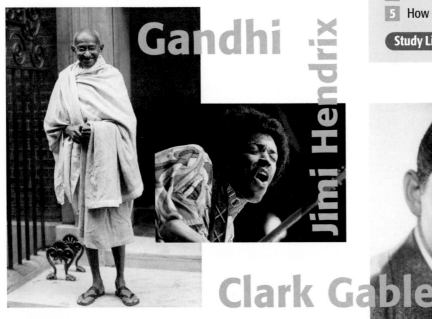

Gandhi

Jimi Hendrix

Clark Gable

Lord Nelson

Study Link www.oup.com/elt/englishfile/elementary

I kissed my first woman and smoked my first cigarette on the same day.
I never had time for tobacco after that.

Arturo Toscanini, Italian conductor

Sydney, here we come!   WORKBOOK

1 PRONUNCIATION -ed endings

a Underline the word where -ed is pronounced /ɪd/.

1 booked   checked   <u>wanted</u>   walked

2 painted   arrived   turned   travelled

3 asked   waited   looked   worked

4 called   played   landed   listened

5 danced   watched   helped   started

6 worked   decided   followed   lived

b Practise saying the words.

2 GRAMMAR past simple regular verbs

a Complete the sentences with a verb, first in the positive and then in the negative.

book	show	help	~~walk~~	play
paint	study	work		

1 Yesterday Sam ___*walked*___ to work, but he
  ___*didn't walk*___ home.

2 I _____ French at school, but I
  _____ German and Spanish.

3 The teacher _____ me with the exercise, but
  she _____ my friend.

4 Bill _____ basketball when he was young, but
  he _____ football.

5 The secretary _____ a table for lunch, but she
  _____ a taxi.

6 We _____ the living room, but we
  _____ the bedroom.

7 The shop assistant _____ last Saturday, but she
  _____ on Sunday.

8 I _____ the photos to my sister, but I
  _____ them to my brother.

b Order the words to make questions.

1 after / Peter / match / tired / Was / the

  A *Was Peter tired after the match?*

  B Yes, he was.

2 you / night / Where / last / were

  A _____?

  B I was at home.

3 they / concert / late / the / Were / for

  A _____?

  B No, they weren't.

4 did / land / the / Where / they / plane

  A _____?

  B At the airport.

5 did / university / your / at / brother / What / study

  A _____?

  B Modern Languages.

6 Was / tall / boyfriend / very / your / first

  A _____?

  B No, not very.

7 didn't / the / you / wait / Why / for / bus

  A _____?

  B Because it was too cold.

8 time / work / did / What / arrive / Sandra / yesterday / at

  A _____?

  B At ten o'clock.

c Complete the questions and answers.

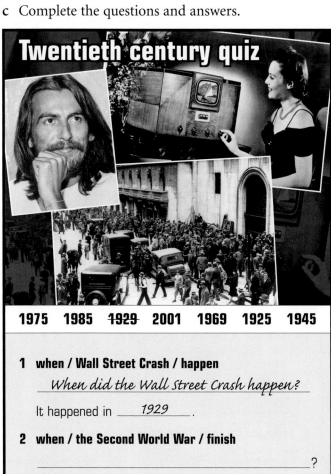

Twentieth century quiz

| 1975 | 1985 | ~~1929~~ | 2001 | 1969 | 1925 | 1945 |

1 when / Wall Street Crash / happen

When did the Wall Street Crash happen?

It happened in ____1929____.

2 when / the Second World War / finish

_____?

It finished in _____.

3 when / Neil Armstrong / land / on the moon

_____?

He landed on the moon in _____.

4 when / mobile phones / first / appear

_____?

They first appeared in _____.

5 when / John Logie Baird / invent the television

_____?

He invented the television in _____.

6 when / George Harrison / die

_____?

He died in _____.

7 when / Bill Gates / start Microsoft

_____?

He started Microsoft in _____.

Study Link Student's Book p.130 *Grammar Bank 5B*

3 VOCABULARY past time expressions

Circle the correct answer.

1 She wasn't in (last night) / yesterday night.

2 My son was born **ago two years** / **two years ago**.

3 They travelled to the USA **last month** / **the last month**.

4 Did you phone me **last morning** / **yesterday morning**?

5 The plane landed **two hours ago** / **two ago hours**.

6 Marc arrived in England **the last July** / **last July**.

7 I stayed with him **before two weeks** / **two weeks ago**.

8 Isabella booked the tickets **yesterday afternoon** / **last afternoon**.

More Words to Learn

Write translations and try to remember the words.

Word	Pronunciation	Translation
<u>tee</u>nager *noun*	/ˈtiːneɪdʒə/	
<u>jou</u>rney *noun*	/ˈdʒɜːni/	
flight *noun*	/flaɪt/	
<u>lu</u>cky *adjective*	/ˈlʌki/	
<u>wo</u>rried *adjective*	/ˈwʌrid/	
book (a ticket) *verb*	/bʊk/	
show *verb*	/ʃəʊ/	
a<u>rrive</u> *verb*	/əˈraɪv/	
land *verb*	/lænd/	
so *conjunction*	/səʊ/	

QUESTION TIME ❓

Can you answer these questions?

1 Did you study English yesterday?

2 Did you watch TV last night?

3 Did you travel by plane last year?

4 Did you cook dinner yesterday?

5 Did you start learning English a year ago?

Study Link MultiROM

Girls' night out

1 VOCABULARY *go, have, get*

a Cross out the wrong expression.

1 GO   to the beach   out   swimming   ~~a bus~~

2 HAVE   lunch   a sandwich   for a walk   a drink

3 GET   dressed   a good time   up   a letter

4 GO   to bed   a taxi   away   to church

5 HAVE   breakfast   a drink   a shower   18 years

6 GET   shopping   home   a newspaper   a taxi

b Complete the spaces in the story with *went*, *had*, or *got*.

Last month Jill, a journalist from London, ¹___*went*___ to Brighton for the weekend. She booked a hotel on the Internet, and on Friday she ²_____ the train to the coast. It was quite late when she arrived, so she just ³_____ a ham and cheese sandwich and ⁴_____ to bed. The next morning she ⁵_____ up early and looked out of the window – it was raining! She ⁶_____ a shower and ⁷_____ dressed, and then she ⁸_____ out to buy some postcards. Another hotel guest ⁹_____ an umbrella and asked her if she needed it. They ¹⁰_____ to the shop together and after that they ¹¹_____ breakfast in a café. From that moment, Jill didn't think about the rain – she ¹²_____ a very good time in Brighton!

Study Link **Student's Book p.150** *Vocabulary Bank*

2 GRAMMAR past simple irregular verbs

a Write sentences in the past.

1 Robert wears a tie to work. (yesterday)
   Robert wore a tie to work yesterday.

2 They do their homework together. (last night)
   _____.

3 Helen doesn't go to the shops. (last week)
   _____.

4 We meet in the bar. (last night)
   _____.

5 We don't have dinner at home. (last night)
   _____.

6 Jane gets up early. (yesterday morning)
   _____.

7 He buys a newspaper at the station. (yesterday)
   _____.

8 I leave home at 7.00. (yesterday)
   _____.

9 She sees her friends after work. (last night)
   _____.

10 Bob can't come to dinner. (last week)
   _____.

b Complete the questions in the dialogue.

A Where ¹___*did you go*___ last night?

B I went to that new jazz club in town.

A ²_____ good?

B Yes, it was great.

A Who ³_____ with?

B I went with my boyfriend and some friends.

A What ⁴_____ ?

B I wore my long denim skirt and a new top I bought last week.

A What time ⁵_____ home?

B We got home at about 3.00 in the morning.

A ⁶_____ a taxi home?

B No, my boyfriend has a car.

A Did ⁷_____ a good time?

B Yes, we had a really great time. You can come with us next time, if you like.

A It depends. ⁸_____ the jazz club expensive?

B No, not very.

Study Link Student's Book p.130 *Grammar Bank 5C*

3 READING

a Read the story.

THE WRONG BUS

A Japanese businessman had a big surprise last Sunday when he got the wrong bus to the airport and missed his flight.

Zenko Kajiyama, 32, went to Waverley station to catch the bus to Edinburgh airport. He had a meeting the next day in London and he wanted to catch the evening flight. When he saw a silver bus marked Club Class he got on it. Unfortunately the bus was for people going to a birthday party.

The people on the bus helped Mr Kajiyama with his bags and found him a seat. He thought he was on the right bus until they stopped at a pub and everyone got off. They asked Mr Kajiyama to join their party and so he followed them into the pub. When he looked at his watch he saw it was too late and that he had missed his plane. At first he was very worried, but then he decided to stay in the pub. He had a drink and danced to the music with the other members of the party. In the end he went back to the house of one of his new friends and he slept on the sofa. The next morning he took a taxi to the airport and flew to London, but he was too late for his meeting.

(adapted from a website)

---

b Mark the sentences T (True) or F (False).

1 Mr Kajiyama wanted to catch the bus to London.   *F*

2 He wanted to go to a party in London.   ___

3 The Club Class bus didn't go to the airport.   ___

4 Mr Kajiyama went to the pub.   ___

5 He didn't catch his plane.   ___

6 In the end he enjoyed the party.   ___

7 He slept in the airport.   ___

8 He didn't go to his meeting in London.   ___

4 PRONUNCIATION past simple irregular verbs

a Circle the word with a different vowel sound.

æ	ɒ	ɔː	eɪ	e
swam	cost	bought	ate	met
came	wrote	saw	made	left
sang	got	heard	said	fell
sat	hot	called	paid	knew

b Practise saying the words.

More Words to Learn

Write translations and try to remember the words.

Word	Pronunciation	Translation
make up *noun*	/'meɪk ʌp/	
cake *noun*	/keɪk/	
wine *noun*	/waɪn/	
dress *noun*	/dres/	
fashions *noun*	/'fæʃənz/	
literature *noun*	/'lɪtrətʃə/	
great (= fantastic) *adjective*	/greɪt/	
open / closed *adjectives*	/'əʊpən/ /kləʊzd/	
pay for *verb*	/'peɪ fə/	
especially *adverb*	/ɪ'speʃəli/	

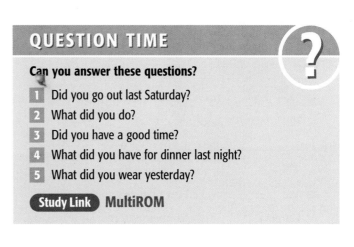

QUESTION TIME

Can you answer these questions?

1 Did you go out last Saturday?

2 What did you do?

3 Did you have a good time?

4 What did you have for dinner last night?

5 What did you wear yesterday?

Study Link MultiROM

Study Link www.oup.com/elt/englishfile/elementary

45

5 D Murder in a country house WORKBOOK

1 PRONUNCIATION past simple verbs

a Match the verbs with the same vowel sound.

| drove | could | ~~made~~ | said | learnt | bought | had | lost |

1	came	_made_		5	saw	_____
2	left	_____		6	spoke	_____
3	got	_____		7	took	_____
4	ran	_____		8	heard	_____

b Practise saying the words.

2 VOCABULARY irregular verbs

a Complete the infinitive and past forms of these irregular verbs. Use *a, e, i, o,* or *u.*

Infinitive	Past		Infinitive	Past
beg _i_ n	beg _a_ n		p_t	p_t
c_me	c_me		r_ng	r_ng
dr_nk	dr_nk		s_t	s_t
dr_ve	dr_ve		w_ke up	w_ke up
g_ve	g_ve		w_n	w_n
kn_w	kn_w		wr_te	wr_te

b Complete the sentences with the past simple form of the verbs in the box.

| buy | find | ~~hear~~ | make | ~~get~~ | not take |
| can't | go | lose | meet | think | |

1 He ___got___ up in the middle of the night because he ___heard___ a noise.

2 I _____ Sally at a party last week.

3 They _____ a new car two days ago.

4 We _____ to bed very late last night.

5 Karen _____ the dinner yesterday. It was pasta, as usual.

6 She was ill, so she _____ her dog for a walk this morning.

7 When we arrived in Paris, we _____ a cheap hotel near the station.

8 The match was a disaster. Our team _____ .

9 I _____ she was Italian, but she was Spanish.

10 I looked everywhere but I _____ find my glasses.

Study Link **Student's Book p.154** *Irregular verbs*

3 GRAMMAR past simple

a Read this police report. Complete the sentences with the past simple form of the verbs in the box.

| be (x2) | ~~arrive~~ | leave | not want | see | can't |
| go | not run | look | open | find | take |

Police report: bank robbery

We ¹ _arrived_ at the bank at 9.36 in the evening, and we ² _____ our police car outside. The bank ³ _____ closed and all the lights ⁴ _____ off, but we ⁵ _____ through the window. We ⁶ _____ a person inside the bank. At first we ⁷ _____ see who it was, but then he ⁸ _____ the door and came out – it was Steven Potter. He ⁹ _____ away – he just walked slowly to his car, and then drove away. The next morning, we ¹⁰ _____ to his house at 6.00 a.m. We ¹¹ _____ him in bed. He ¹² _____ to speak to us, so we ¹³ _____ him to the police station.

b Complete the questions with the correct form of the verbs in brackets.

POLICE OFFICER Where ¹_____*were you*_____ at about 9.30 yesterday evening? (be)

STEVEN POTTER I was at the cinema. The film started at 9.00.

PO What film ²_____? (see)

SP I can't remember. It wasn't very good.

PO Hmm. Very interesting. And who ³_____ to the cinema with? (go)

SP With my girlfriend.

PO ⁴_____ the film? (like)

SP Yes, she thought it was very good.

PO What time ⁵_____ the film _____? (finish)

SP At about 10.30.

PO And what ⁶_____ after you left the cinema? (do)

SP We went to a restaurant – *La Dolce Vita*, on the High Street.

PO *La Dolce Vita*? I know it. Very good spaghetti. What time ⁷_____ the restaurant? (leave)

SP At about 12.00.

PO That's very late. ⁸_____ home after that? (go)

SP No, we went to a nightclub – *Flanagan's*. Then we went home.

PO How? ⁹_____ a taxi? (get)

SP No, we got a bus.

PO And what time ¹⁰_____ to bed? (go)

SP At about 4.00 a.m. Can I go home now? I'm tired.

PO No, I'd like to ask you some more questions…

More Words to Learn

Write translations and try to remember the words.

Word	Pronunciation	Translation
<u>c</u>ountry <u>house</u> *noun*	/ˈkʌntri ˈhaʊs/	
milli<u>onaire</u> *noun*	/mɪljəˈneə/	
<u>li</u>brary *noun*	/ˈlaɪbri/	
<u>mur</u>der *noun*	/ˈmɜːdə/	
a<u>sleep</u> *adjective*	/əˈsliːp/	
dead *adjective*	/ded/	
<u>hap</u>pen *verb*	/ˈhæpən/	
<u>e</u>verybody *pronoun*	/ˈevribɒdi/	
<u>so</u>mebody *pronoun*	/ˈsʌmbɒdi/	
<u>no</u>body *pronoun*	/ˈnəʊbɒdi/	

QUESTION TIME   ?

Can you answer these questions?

1 What time did you get up yesterday?

2 Where were you at 2 o'clock?

3 Where did you go after lunch?

4 Did you go out in the evening?

5 What time did you go to bed?

Study Link MultiROM

CAN YOU REMEMBER…?   **FILES 4&5**

Complete each space with one word.

1 A _____ your daughter swim?

  B Yes, but not very well.

2 Do you like _____ to the gym?

3 We help them and they help _____.

4 A Whose is this car?

  B It's _____. We bought it last week.

5 Where _____ you born?

6 I _____ go out last night. I was very tired.

7 Did you _____ a good time at the party?

8 We _____ to a really good restaurant last night.

1 VOCABULARY shopping

Write the words.

1 _postcards_   3 a m_____   5 b_____

2 f_____   4 T-_____

2 BUYING A PRESENT

Order the dialogue.

A Next, please.   ☐ 1

B No thanks. Just the mug.   ☐

A It's £5.   ☐

B How much is a large mug?   ☐

A These mugs are quite cheap.   ☐

B How much are the T-shirts?   ☐ 2

B Red, please.   ☐

A Red or blue?   ☐

B Oh! They're very expensive!   ☐

A Here you are. Anything else?   ☐

A They're £30.   ☐

B OK. Can I have a mug, please? ☐

3 SOCIAL ENGLISH

Complete the dialogue with these words.

believe	Come	look	nice	problem
Relax	time	~~Wow~~		

A Hi Sally. [1] _Wow_ ! You [2]_____ great. Nice dress!

B Here's a little present for you.

A That's very [3]_____ of you. Oh no, it's broken.

B I don't [4]_____ it! I'm sorry, Carl.

A No [5]_____. What time did you book the restaurant for?

B For 8 o'clock. [6]_____ on. It's [7]_____ to go. It's late.

A [8]_____ Sally. We have time. We can get a taxi.

4 READING

a Complete the text with these words.

biscuits	love	cup	~~shops~~	find	popular

Souvenirs from Britain

What do visitors to Britain take home as a souvenir? We visited twenty souvenir [1] _shops_ in London, and this is what we found…

Tea and biscuits

The British love their tea, and tourists seem to love it too. You can buy it in tins and boxes, and in many different varieties. And why not buy a [2]_____ or a mug with a picture of the Houses of Parliament at the same time? And to have with your tea – what about some [3]_____ from Scotland, or some traditional sweets and chocolate?

Postcards and pictures

Postcards and pictures of famous sights are very [4]_____ souvenirs. Big Ben? The Tower of London? Piccadilly Circus? You can [5]_____ all these, and a lot of other places too! Tourists also buy paintings and photos of the beautiful British countryside, especially the Scottish Highlands.

The royal family

The royal family have their problems, but tourists still [6]_____ them. Souvenir shops are full of royal mugs, tea towels, postcards, teddy bears, T-shirts, and teapots.

b Underline five words or phrases you don't know. Use your dictionary to look up their meaning and pronunciation.

6 A house with a history

1 VOCABULARY flats and houses

a Write the room.

study	~~hall~~	dining room
bedroom	living room	kitchen
garage	bathroom	

Where do you usually…

1 … take off your coat? In the ___hall___ .

2 … have a shower? In the _____.

3 … have dinner? In the _____.

4 … use a computer? In the _____.

5 … park your car? In the _____.

6 … make lunch? In the _____.

7 … watch television? In the _____.

8 … sleep? In the _____.

b Complete the crossword.

2 GRAMMAR there is / there are

a Complete with the correct form of *there is / there are* and, if necessary, *a*, *some*, or *any*.

A Could you give me some more information about the house?

B Of course. What do you want to know?

A [1] ____*Is there a*____ garden?

B Yes, [2] _____ large garden, with a swimming pool.

A Oh, very nice! And how many bedrooms [3] _____?

B Three, I think…yes, [4] _____ three bedrooms.

A And [5] _____ dining room?

B No, [6] _____. But [7] _____ big kitchen.

A [8] _____ shelves in the kitchen?

B No, [9] _____. But [10] _____ cupboards. Do you have any more questions?

A Yes. The furniture… [11] _____ armchairs in the living room?

B No, I'm sorry. [12] _____ armchairs, but [13] _____ sofa.

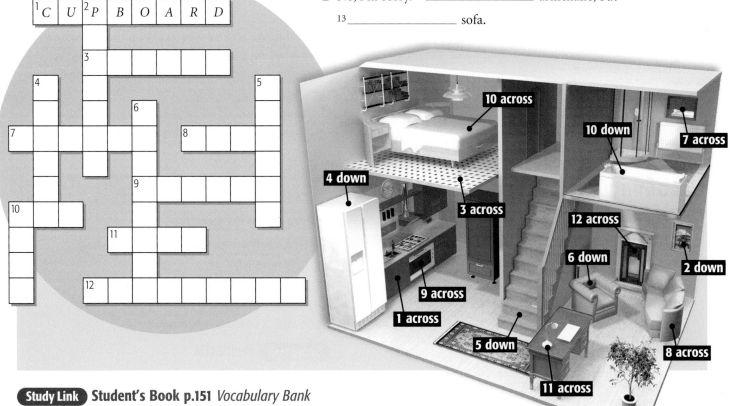

1 C U 2 P B O A R D

b Write the sentences in the plural.

1 There's a cigarette on the floor.

There are some cigarettes on the floor.

2 Is there a plant in your living room?

_____ ?

3 There's a key in that door.

_____ .

4 Is there a toilet in this restaurant?

_____ ?

5 There isn't a window in this room.

_____ .

c Circle the correct form.

¹(It's)/ **There's** a very nice house. ² **There's / It's** a large garden, and ³ **there are / they are** some trees in the garden. I think ⁴ **there are / they are** apple trees. ⁵ **There's / It's** a living room, with a big blue sofa. In the kitchen, ⁶ **there aren't / they aren't** any shelves, but ⁷ **there are / they are** some cupboards. ⁸ **There are / They are** quite old, but the fridge and cooker are new. And the bathroom's fantastic – ⁹ **there isn't / it isn't** very big, but ¹⁰ **there's / it's** a shower and a bath!

Study Link **Student's Book p.132** *Grammar Bank 6A*

3 PRONUNCIATION /ð/ and /eə/, word stress

a Circle the word with a different sound.

ð	θ	eə	ɪə
brother	thirsty	here	engineer
(think)	thing	hair	wear
then	that	where	near
together	thanks	stairs	beer

b Underline the stressed syllable. Which two words are not stressed on the first syllable?

1 <u>car</u>pet   4 fantastic   7 armchair

2 mirror   5 cooker   8 information

3 cupboard   6 sofa

c Practise saying the words in **a** and **b**.

More Words to Learn

Write translations and try to remember the words.

Word	Pronunciation	Translation
<u>price</u> *noun*	/praɪs/	
<u>paint</u>ings *noun*	/ˈpeɪntɪŋz/	
<u>es</u>tate agent *noun*	/ɪˈsteɪt ˈeɪdʒənt/	
plants *noun*	/plɑːnts/	
large *adjective*	/lɑːdʒ/	
<u>qui</u>et *adjective*	/ˈkwaɪət/	
<u>lo</u>cal (pub) *adjective*	/ˈləʊkl/	
o<u>ri</u>ginal *adjective*	/əˈrɪdʒənl/	
rent *verb*	/rent/	
draw *verb*	/drɔː/	

Study idea

Irregular verbs

1 When you learn new verbs, check in the dictionary to see if they are regular or irregular in the past tense.

2 If they are irregular, write IRR next to the verb in your vocabulary notebook, and write the past simple form next to it too.

3 Look up *rent* and *draw* in your dictionary. Which one is irregular? What's the past simple form?

QUESTION TIME ?

Can you answer these questions?

1 How many bedrooms are there in your house?
2 Is there a study?
3 Is there a computer in your living room?
4 Are there any plants in your kitchen?
5 Is there a sofa in your bedroom?

Study Link **MultiROM**

50

I'm not frightened of death. I just don't want to be there when it happens.
Woody Allen, American film director

A night in a haunted hotel   **WORKBOOK**

1 VOCABULARY prepositions of place

Complete the sentences with these words.

over	~~in~~	between	on	in front of
in	behind	next to	under	opposite

1 There's a big table _____*in*_____ the room.

2 There's a small table _____ the door.

3 There's a black dog _____ the table.

4 A cat is sitting _____ the fireplace.

5 There's a ghost sitting _____ the woman.

6 Another ghost is standing _____ the woman.

7 There are some glasses _____ the cupboard.

8 There are some plates _____ the table.

9 There's a picture _____ the fireplace.

10 There's a sofa _____ the two armchairs.

2 GRAMMAR there was / there were

a Complete the text. Use *was, were, wasn't,* or *weren't.*

I went on holiday to Greece last month. I stayed in a really nice hotel – there ¹ _*were*_ two swimming pools in the garden! There ² _____ a small beach in front of the hotel. There ³ _____ any cars on the road, but there ⁴ _____ some buses, and a lot of tourists. There ⁵ _____ a restaurant in the hotel, but there ⁶ _____ some very nice restaurants in the town. There ⁷ _____ a waiter called Manolis – he was very friendly. There ⁸ _____ a big window, so I could see the sea. In the evening, when there ⁹ _____ any people on the beach, it was very beautiful.

b Complete the dialogue.

A Did you have a nice holiday in Greece?

B Yes, it was great. The hotel was really nice.

A Was it? ¹ _*Was*_ _*there*_ a swimming pool?

B Yes, ² _____ _____ two swimming pools.

A Two swimming pools! Wow! What about your room?

B ³ _____ _____ a big bed, but ⁴ _____ _____ a television. ⁵ _____ _____ a minibar, and a beautiful sofa next to the window.

A ⁶ _____ _____ any other British tourists?

B No, ⁷ _____ _____. But ⁸ _____ _____ some Italians and some Germans.

A ⁹ _____ _____ a restaurant in the hotel?

B No, ¹⁰ _____ _____. But ¹¹ _____ _____ some nice restaurants in the town, near the beach.

Study Link **Student's Book p.132** *Grammar Bank 6B*

3 READING

a Read the advert.

Castle to rent

This beautiful 17th-century castle in the Lot Valley
in southern France has 25 hectares of land.
The owners live in the east wing of the castle
and rent the rest of the building to tourists.

In front of the main entrance to the castle there's a
rose garden and a pretty fountain , which is lit up at
night. In the back garden there's a heated swimming
pool with a wonderful terrace for sunbathing .

There's room in the castle for 20 people to sleep.
There are 10 bedrooms on the first and second floors, all
of which have a television, and there are six bathrooms.
There's a large formal dining room on the ground floor,
where eight people can eat, and there's a dining area
outside where all 20 guests can have dinner together.
For relaxing in the evening, there's a large living room
with sofas and armchairs. Downstairs there's also a study
and a very spacious kitchen with doors to the garden.

The house is cleaned twice a week and there is a
babysitting service.

(adapted from a website)

b Read the advert again and answer the questions.

1 How old is the castle?

2 Who lives in the castle?

3 What two things can you do in the back garden?

4 How many bedrooms are there?

5 Where can 20 guests eat together?

6 How often do people come to clean the house?

c Guess the meaning of the highlighted words.
Check with your dictionary.

4 PRONUNCIATION silent letters

a Cross out the silent consonants.

1	ghost	6	could
2	autumn	7	write
3	comb	8	half
4	listen	9	cupboard
5	white	10	hour

b Practise saying the words.

More Words to Learn

Write translations and try to remember the words.

Word	Pronunciation	Translation
ghost *noun*	/gəʊst/	
century *noun*	/ˈsentʃəri/	
priest *noun*	/priːst/	
guest *noun*	/gest/	
nervous *adjective*	/ˈnɜːvəs/	
frightened *adjective*	/ˈfraɪtnd/	
strange *adjective*	/streɪndʒ/	
believe *verb*	/bɪˈliːv/	
go back *verb*	/gəʊ ˈbæk/	
spend (the night) *verb*	/spend/	

QUESTION TIME

Can you answer these questions?

1 Where's the TV in your house?

2 What building is opposite your school?

3 How many people were there in your last English class?

4 Was there a good film on TV last night?

5 Was there a festival in your town last month?

Study Link MultiROM

Hell is other people.
Jean-Paul Sartre, French philosopher

1 VOCABULARY verb phrases

Complete the text with these verbs, in the correct form.

~~argue~~ move bark cry talk have watch play

My neighbours, Mr and Mrs Jackson, are terrible. They
¹ _argue_ all the time and their dog ² _____ all day. They
have a three-month-old baby who ³ _____ every night,
and Mr Jackson ⁴ _____ the violin early in the morning.
Then Mrs Jackson gets up, and they ⁵ _____ loudly
about everything. In the evening, they often ⁶ _____ their
furniture around and they ⁷ _____ TV late at night. And
at the weekends, they often ⁸ _____ noisy parties!

2 GRAMMAR present continuous

a Complete the dialogue.

A What ¹ _____are you doing_____ (you / do), Granny?

B I ² _____ (look) at the neighbours.

A What ³ _____ (they / do)?

⁴ _____ (Mrs Jackson / watch) TV?

B No, she ⁵ _____ (move) the furniture.

A And ⁶ _____ (Mr Jackson / play)

the violin?

B Yes, he is. Oh, look! Some people

⁷ _____ (arrive). I think they want to

have a party. Mr Jackson ⁸ _____

(open) the door…

b Look at the picture of a park. What are the people
doing?

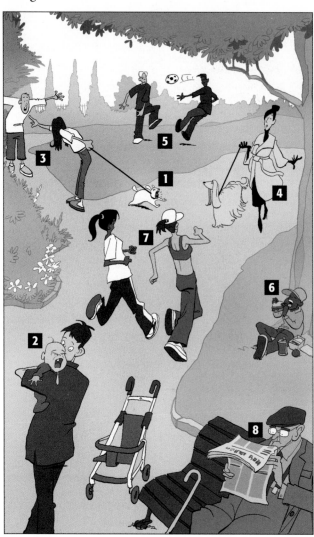

1 *The dog's barking.*

2 _____ .

3 _____ .

4 _____ .

5 _____ .

6 _____ .

7 _____ .

8 _____ .

Study Link **Student's Book p.132** *Grammar Bank 6C*

3 READING

a Read the text.

Noisy neighbours

Do you have problems with your neighbours? Well, imagine the problems the people of Pilton in Somerset, England, have. Every summer over 150,000 people travel to their village for the annual Glastonbury pop music festival.

Every year, for three days, the village is full of people of all ages who leave drinks cans and papers all over the streets. The music plays until the early hours of the morning and you can hear people talking and singing all night. The quiet country village becomes a nightmare to live in and some residents are even thinking of moving to another village.

The pop fans who go to Glastonbury usually sleep in tents in a field, but last year Mr James Findlay, a resident of Pilton, found two people asleep in his garden in the morning. Mr Findlay said, 'I don't want to stop the Glastonbury Festival. I just want the fans to enjoy the festival without disturbing normal village life.'

(adapted from a website)

b Tick ☑ the problems the villagers of Pilton have with their temporary neighbours.

1 ☐ Their dogs bark.
2 ☐ They throw their rubbish in the streets.
3 ☐ They listen to loud music.
4 ☐ Their babies cry all night.
5 ☐ They make a lot of noise.
6 ☐ They go into other people's gardens.
7 ☐ They watch TV late at night.
8 ☐ They break things in the village.

c Guess the meaning of the highlighted words. Check with your dictionary.

4 PRONUNCIATION verb + -ing

a Circle the word with a different sound.

🐟	drinking	(writing)	swimming	giving
iː	meeting	reading	speaking	hearing
ɔɪ	talking	walking	working	calling
eɪ	playing	having	raining	painting
əʊ	knowing	going	doing	closing
aɪ	living	buying	finding	riding

b Practise saying the words.

More Words to Learn

Write translations and try to remember the words.

Word	Pronunciation	Translation
neighbour *noun*	/ˈneɪbə/	
violin *noun*	/vaɪəˈlɪn/	
baby *noun*	/ˈbeɪbi/	
noisy *adjective*	/ˈnɔɪzi/	
friendly *adjective*	/ˈfrendli/	
choose *verb*	/tʃuːz/	
argue *verb*	/ˈɑːgjuː/	
cry *verb*	/kraɪ/	
bark *verb*	/bɑːk/	
move *verb*	/muːv/	

When a man is tired of London, he is tired of life.
Samuel Johnson, English writer

When a man is tired of London... WORKBOOK

1 GRAMMAR present simple or present continuous?

a Circle the correct form.

1 **A** What do you do / (What are you doing) here?

B I'm waiting for a friend.

2 **Do you walk / Are you walking** to work every day?

3 Barbara isn't here. She **buys / 's buying** a present for her daughter.

4 I **go / 'm going** to work now. See you later.

5 It **rains / 's raining** a lot here in the winter.

6 **A** Where's Laura?

B She's on the phone. She **'s talking / talks** to Paul.

7 **Does your baby cry / Is your baby crying** at night?

8 My husband **watches / 's watching** football three times a week.

b Complete the sentences. Use the present simple or present continuous.

1 What time _____*does he start*_____ (he / start) work every day?

2 David's in the bathroom. He _____ (have) a shower.

3 **A** Where's Sally?

B She _____ (do) her homework.

4 Peter and Clare _____ (not / like) their neighbours.

5 My parents _____ (look) for a new house at the moment.

6 Lisa usually _____ (cook) the dinner during the week.

7 I _____ (watch) a programme on TV. Can you phone me later?

8 My husband _____ (go) to bed very late – usually at midnight.

9 We _____ (not / want) to drive to Scotland. It's 500 km!

10 **A** Where _____ (you / go)?

B To the bank – see you later.

Study Link Student's Book p.132 *Grammar Bank 6D*

2 VOCABULARY town and city

a Complete the sentences with a word from each box.

police ~~art~~ department sports shopping railway travel

centre station store agent's station centre ~~gallery~~

1 Where can you see paintings?

In an _____*art*_____ _____*gallery*_____.

2 Where can you visit different shops?

At a _____ _____.

3 Where can you get a train from?

From a _____ _____.

4 Where can you book a holiday?

At a _____ _____.

5 Where can you talk to a police officer?

At a _____ _____.

6 Where can you buy clothes for all the family?

In a _____ _____.

7 Where can you play basketball?

At a _____ _____.

b Complete the puzzle.

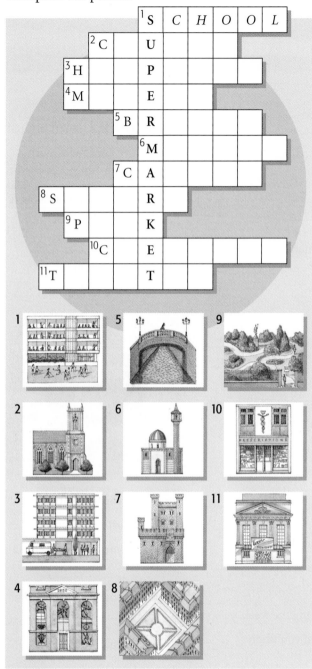

Study Link Student's Book p.152 *Vocabulary Bank*

3 PRONUNCIATION /ə/

a Under<u>li</u>ne the /ə/ sound.

1 cen<u>tre</u>   6 ago

2 shower   7 theatre

3 opposite   8 mirror

4 sofa   9 tomorrow

5 picture   10 parent

b Practise saying the words.

More Words to Learn

Write translations and try to remember the words.

Word	Pronunciation	Translation
ship *noun*	/ʃɪp/	
flag *noun*	/flæg/	
trip *noun*	/trɪp/	
<u>pa</u>ssenger *noun*	/ˈpæsɪndʒə/	
<u>bu</u>ilding *noun*	/ˈbɪldɪŋ/	
view *noun*	/vjuː/	
<u>un</u>derground *noun*	/ˈʌndəɡraʊnd/	
each *determiner*	/iːtʃ/	
through *preposition*	/θruː/	
What a <u>pi</u>ty!	/wɒt ə ˈpɪti/	

QUESTION TIME   ?

Can you answer these questions?

1 What kind of books do you read?

2 What are you reading now?

3 What do you usually wear?

4 What are you wearing now?

5 What's the main tourist attraction in your town?

Study Link MultiROM

CAN YOU REMEMBER...?   FILES 5&6

Complete each space with one word.

1 My grandparents _____ doctors. They died before I was born.

2 _____ they book their holiday on the Internet last summer?

3 We _____ pizza and Coke for lunch yesterday.

4 I _____ see the end of the film because I fell asleep.

5 There _____ two bathrooms in my new house.

6 There _____ many people at the beach yesterday – it was very cold.

7 Listen! The neighbours are _____ a noise again.

8 A _____ you staying at a hotel, or with friends?
   B We're in a little hotel in the town centre.

Study Link www.oup.com/elt/englishfile/elementary

1 VOCABULARY directions

Complete the words and phrases.

1	2	3	4
5	6	7	8

1 on the ___corner___

2 at the t_____

   l_____

3 a r_____

4 o_____

5 turn l_____

6 turn r_____

7 go s_____

   o_____

8 go p_____ the station

2 ASKING FOR DIRECTIONS

Complete the dialogue with these words.

exactly	~~Excuse~~	near	say	first
tell	way	Where's		

A ¹ ___Excuse___ me. ² _____ Barton street, please?

B Sorry, I don't know.

A Excuse me. Is Barton Street ³ _____ here?

C Barton Street? I know the name, but I don't know

   ⁴ _____ where it is. Sorry.

A Excuse me. Can you ⁵ _____ me the

   ⁶ _____ to Barton Street?

D Yes. Turn right at the traffic lights. Then it's the

   ⁷ _____ on the left.

A Sorry, could you ⁸ _____ that again?

3 SOCIAL ENGLISH

Match the phrases.

1 Let's ask that man.   a I'm only joking.

2 You were right.   b He probably knows the way.

3 Excuse me. We're lost.   c It was the second on the left.

4 Don't be angry.   d Could you help us?

4 READING

a   Read the information about getting around London.

> ## Getting around London
>
> ### By underground
> The London Underground, usually called 'the tube', is enormous and can take you everywhere quickly. However, it is hot and uncomfortable in the summer, and can be confusing for tourists, who often get on the wrong train. It can also be very crowded in the 'rush hour' (7.00–9.00 in the morning and 5.00–7.00 in the evening).
>
>
>
> ### By bus
> The buses give you a good view of the sights, especially if you travel upstairs, but if the traffic is bad, your journey can take a long time. Special tickets, called travelcards, can be used on both buses and the underground and are quite economical.
>
> ### By taxi or car
> Taxis are excellent, but very expensive. Never take a car into central London – it's nearly impossible to park, and you also have to pay a congestion charge (currently £5) every time you drive into the centre.

b   Answer the questions.

1 What's another name for the London Underground?

2 When is the underground usually very busy?

3 Where is a good place to sit to see the sights?

4 Where can you use travelcards?

5 What's the problem with taking a taxi?

6 How much do you have to pay if you take your car into the centre of London?

c   Match the highlighted adjectives to their meanings.

very big   ___enormous___   full of people _____

very good   _____   difficult to understand _____

quite cheap   _____

7A

What does your food say about you?

If it tastes good, it's bad for you.
Isaac Asimov, science fiction writer

1 VOCABULARY food

a Complete the crossword.

Clues across →

²C E R E A ³L

Clues down ↓

b Write the words in the correct column.

apples	cake	crisps	~~carrots~~	pineapple
onions	grapes	chocolate	mushrooms	
peas	bananas	biscuits		

Vegetables	Snacks	Fruit
carrots		

Study Link Student's Book p.153 *Vocabulary Bank*

2 GRAMMAR a / an, some / any

a What did Mark and Jan buy when they went shopping yesterday? Write *a, an,* or *some* in the spaces.

1	*some*	meat
2	_____	apple
3	_____	cheese
4	_____	milk
5	_____	butter
6	_____	banana
7	_____	pineapple
8	_____	oranges
9	_____	onion
10	_____	tomatoes

b Write the sentences in positive or negative form.

1 There's some rice in the cupboard.

   There isn't any rice in the cupboard.

2 I _____.

   I didn't eat any fruit yesterday.

3 I _____.

   I didn't have an egg for breakfast.

4 There _____.

   There isn't any sugar in this coffee.

5 We have some vegetables in the garden.

   We _____.

6 There _____.

   There weren't any sandwiches in the fridge.

7 There was some nice fish at the supermarket.

   There _____.

8 I had a salad for lunch.

   I _____.

c Complete the dialogue with *a, an, some,* or *any*.

   A I'm going to the supermarket. Would you like anything?

   B Yes, can you get ¹ *some* milk and ² _____ bottle of wine?

   A But there's ³ _____ milk in the fridge.

B No, there isn't. I drank it this morning. And we need 4_____ bread for sandwiches tomorrow. Oh, yes – do we have 5_____ cheese? I'd like to make 6_____ pizza this evening.

A Yes, I think there's 7_____ cheese in the fridge. And there are 8_____ tomatoes in the cupboard.

B And I'd like 9_____ onion too, please. There aren't 10_____ in the cupboard. Oh, and we need 11_____ eggs…

Study Link Student's Book p.134 *Grammar Bank 7A*

3 PRONUNCIATION the letters *ea*

Circle the word with a different sound. Practise saying the words.

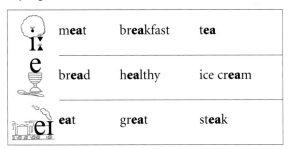

iː	meat	breakfast	**tea**
e	bread	healthy	ice cream
eɪ	eat	great	steak

4 READING

a Match each 'food fact' to the paragraph which explains why it's false.

A Eating too much sugar can make you addicted. ☐

B Beer is good for your hair. ☐

C Eating fruit at the end of a meal is very healthy. ☐

D Putting salt in water will make it boil quicker. 1

More Words to Learn

Write translations and try to remember the words.

Word	Pronunciation	Translation
(shopping) <u>bas</u>ket *noun*	/ˈbɑːskɪt/	
spag<u>h</u>etti *noun*	/spəˈgeti/	
dish *noun*	/dɪʃ/	
in<u>gred</u>ients *noun*	/ɪnˈgriːdɪənts/	
<u>lux</u>ury *noun*	/ˈlʌkʃəri/	
<u>miss</u>ing *adjective*	/ˈmɪsɪŋ/	
<u>coun</u>table *adjective*	/ˈkaʊntəbl/	
un<u>coun</u>table *adjective*	/ʌnˈkaʊntəbl/	

Study idea

1 Try to connect new words with other words in English or in your language, e.g. shopping **basket** – **basket**ball.

2 Look at the words in **More Words to Learn**. Can you connect them to any other words?

QUESTION TIME

Can you answer these questions?

1 What do you usually have for breakfast?

2 What do you drink with your dinner?

3 What's your favourite food?

4 What vegetables don't you like?

5 What do you drink when you go out with your friends?

Study Link MultiROM

Food facts…or are they?

 1 Many cooks always put salt into water before putting in the pasta. Many say that this helps the water boil more quickly, but this isn't true. In fact salt makes water boil at a higher temperature, so the water boils more slowly.

 2 Putting beer on your hair is not a good idea. The only result is a shower that smells like a pub, and hair which looks terrible. It is impossible for the beer to make your hair more beautiful, believe me, so don't try it.

 3 When people eat a lot of sweet things, it isn't because their body really needs sugar. It's because they like the taste, and they often have a lot of sweet things like cakes and biscuits in their cupboards. Sugar is not a drug and eating it is just a bad habit.

 4 Fruit is quite difficult to digest. If you eat it at the end of a meal, it can stay in your stomach for a long time. This means that you can feel very uncomfortable if you've just eaten a very big meal. The best time to eat fruit is between meals.

(adapted from a website)

b Guess the meaning of the highlighted words. Check with your dictionary.

Human beings are 70% water. With some people, the rest is collagen.

Martin Mull, American actor and writer

1 PRONUNCIATION /w/, /v/, and /b/

a William, Vera, and Brenda are thinking about the presents they want for their birthdays. William wants presents that begin with /w/, Vera wants those that begin with /v/, and Brenda wants those that begin with /b/. What presents do they each want?

W	**V**	**b**
William	Vera	Brenda
wine	_____	_____
_____	_____	_____
_____	_____	_____
_____		

b Practise saying the words.

2 GRAMMAR *how much / how many?*, quantifiers

a Complete the questions. Then complete the sentences.

1 *He doesn't smoke many cigarettes.*

2 He _____ .

3 She _____ .

4 He _____ .

5 She _____ .

6 She _____ .

b Read about these records in competitive eating.

Competitive eating

	Alina Baden ate 46 hot dogs in 11 minutes.
	George Willis ate 128 chicken wings in 28 minutes.
	Nikolai Cohen ate 10 hamburgers in 11 minutes.
	John Edwards ate 7 litres of ice-cream in 14 minutes.
	Gustav Sajer drank 6 litres of milk in 3 minutes 29 seconds.
	Barbara Beard ate 5 kilos of fruit (bananas and apples) in 9 minutes 15 seconds.

Write questions.

1 *How many hamburgers did Nikolai Cohen eat?*
   Ten.

2 _____?
   Six litres.

3 _____?
   Seven litres.

4 _____?
   A hundred and twenty-eight.

5 _____?
   Five kilos.

6 _____?
   Forty-six.

Study Link **Student's Book p.134** *Grammar Bank 7B*

3 VOCABULARY drinks

Write the names of the drinks.

1 *beer*   4 _____   7 _____
2 _____   5 _____   8 _____
3 _____   6 _____

4 VOCABULARY 'water' reading

Complete the sentences with these words.

temperature	at least	~~sweat~~	contain
experiments	in fact	myth	

1 When you're hot, you __*sweat*__ to reduce your body heat.

2 We don't always need to drink a lot of water. _____ sometimes one litre a day is OK.

3 The _____ in Madrid in August is very high.

4 Scientists are doing _____ to find a cure for the common cold.

5 Sweets and chocolate _____ a lot of calories.

6 Some people say you need to drink _____ two litres of water a day.

7 It's a _____ that coffee and Coke make you thirsty – it's just not true!

More Words to Learn

Write translations and try to remember the words.

Word	Pronunciation	Translation
<u>li</u>tres *noun*	/ˈliːtəz/	
tap *noun*	/tæp/	
lose *verb*	/luːz/	
a<u>gree</u> *verb*	/əˈgriː/	
<u>pro</u>bably *adverb*	/ˈprɒbəbli/	
like *preposition*	/laɪk/	
a <u>bott</u>le of…	/ə ˈbɒtl əv/	
of <u>course</u>	/əv ˈkɔːs/	
<u>more</u> or <u>less</u>	/ˈmɔː(r) ə ˈles/	
for e<u>xam</u>ple	/fə ɪgˈzɑːmpl/	

QUESTION TIME ?

Can you answer these questions?

1 How much water do you usually drink?
2 How many cigarettes do you smoke?
3 How much television do you watch?
4 How much money do you spend on clothes?
5 How many very good friends do you have?

Study Link MultiROM

1 GRAMMAR *be going to* (plans)

a Order the words to make sentences.

1 going / She / holiday / enjoy / 's / the / to
She's going to enjoy the holiday.

2 to / aren't / We / a / going / stay / in / hotel

_____ .

3 going / They / to / go / 're / swimming

_____ .

4 'm / I / go / camping / going / to

_____ .

5 you / to / Are / trip / for / going / pay / the

_____ ?

6 isn't / see / the / He / to / going / pyramids

_____ .

b Complete the sentences. Use *going to*.

1 What time ___are they going to leave___ (they / leave) tomorrow?

2 We _____ (try) the local food.

3 They _____ (have) dinner with their friends this weekend.

4 _____ (you / stay) at an expensive hotel?

5 They _____ (not / get married) until next year.

6 _____ (they / see) the Statue of Liberty?

7 He _____ (meet) a lot of people.

8 She _____ (not / go) on holiday this year.

c Complete the dialogue. Use *going to*.

A So, where ¹ *are you going to go* (go) on holiday?

B We ² _____ _____ (travel) round Europe by train.

A That sounds great. Which countries ³ _____ (visit)?

B Italy first, and then Croatia, Greece, and Turkey.

A Where ⁴ _____ (sleep)?

B Well, we ⁵ _____ (not / stay) in hotels! We don't have much money. We can sleep on the train. The only problem is that it ⁶ _____ (be) very hot.

A And where ⁷ _____ (go) after Italy?

B After Italy we ⁸ _____ (get) the train to Zagreb. Then Makiko ⁹ _____ (come) home and I ¹⁰ _____ (go) to Greece. I want to visit Athens and then I ¹¹ _____ (spend) a week on a Greek island before I go to Turkey. I ¹² _____ (not / get) home until the end of August.

Study Link **Student's Book p.134** *Grammar Bank 7C*

2 PRONUNCIATION word stress

a Underline the stressed syllable in these words. How many are not stressed on the first syllable?

1 <u>ho</u>liday	4 weather	7 nightlife
2 hotel	5 museum	8 programme
3 campsite	6 restaurant	

b Practise saying the words.

3 VOCABULARY holidays

Write the expressions in the correct column.

on holiday   the sights   ~~in a hotel~~   shopping
to the beach   at a campsite   in a bed and breakfast
a show   the Statue of Liberty

STAY	GO	SEE
in a hotel		

4 READING

a Read the adverts.

★ Four *dream* holidays for the 21st century

A ★ See a penguin

This is a once-in-a-lifetime holiday in the snow and ice of the Antarctic. You visit the isolated places the great explorers discovered and you can see animals and birds you only normally see on TV or in zoos. The trip starts in South Africa and finishes in Western Australia. You travel on a Russian ship, *Kapitan Khlebnikov*, and the holiday lasts for just under a month.

B ★ Go on safari

This holiday is a safari with a difference. You travel by helicopter over parts of Kenya, listening to classical music as you fly, and then you sleep under the African stars in a luxury bed. There's another trip, this time in a hot-air balloon for two people, which gives you a second chance to see wild animals in their natural habitat. The best moment is the Elephant Watch in Samburu, where your experienced guide can tell you all about these amazing animals.

C ★ Fly high

This is probably the most expensive holiday in the world. You can go on a flight into space and orbit the Earth in a spaceship – if you have the money! The only problem with this holiday is the six-day training course before you take the trip. You travel 60 miles above the Earth for between 30 and 90 minutes and you get a beautiful view of our green and blue planet.

D ★ Live like Robinson Crusoe

If you dream of life on a desert island, then this is the holiday for you. The island of Quilalea is off the coast of Mozambique and the only inhabitants are turtles and a few tourists. You can live like Robinson Crusoe: watch the turtles, go fishing, or sail to another island to have a picnic.

(adapted from a website)

b Read the text again and match the tourists to a holiday.

1 A millionaire looking for something to tell his friends.

2 A rich couple who like animals and hot weather.

3 A strong young scientist who enjoys cold weather.

4 A group of friends who want to forget about their stressful jobs.

c Read the text again and label the pictures.

1 _*penguin*_   2 _____   3 _____

4 _____   5 _____   6 _____

More Words to Learn

Write translations and try to remember the words.

Word	Pronunciation	Translation
<u>c</u>ouple *noun*	/ˈkʌpl/	
<u>m</u>oment *noun*	/ˈməʊmənt/	
(see the) <u>s</u>ights *noun*	/saɪts/	
<u>cam</u>psite *noun*	/ˈkæmpsaɪt/	
<u>night</u>life *noun*	/ˈnaɪtlaɪf/	
di<u>sa</u>ster *noun*	/dɪˈzɑːstə/	
boat *noun*	/bəʊt/	
<u>ide</u>al *adjective*	/aɪˈdɪːəl/	
plan *verb*	/plæn/	
go <u>cam</u>ping *verb*	/ˈkæmpɪŋ/	

QUESTION TIME

Can you answer these questions?

1 Where are you going to go on holiday this year?

2 What are you going to see there?

3 What are you going to do there?

4 Who are you going to go with?

5 How much is it going to cost you?

Study Link MultiROM

It's written in the cards

1 VOCABULARY verb phrases

Complete with verbs from the box. Sometimes more than one answer is possible.

be	have	get	fall	move	meet

1 _be_ famous
2 _____ a surprise
3 _____ married
4 _____ lucky
5 _____ in love
6 _____ to another country
7 _____ a lot of money
8 _____ house
9 _____ a new job
10 _____ somebody new
11 _____ a baby

2 GRAMMAR be going to (predictions)

a Look at the picture and write sentences using these verbs and *be going to*.

buy	~~eat~~	take	fall	get	have	make	see

1 _____She's going to eat_____ her ice cream.
2 _____ off his bike.
3 _____ a taxi.
4 _____ a cigarette.
5 _____ a film.
6 _____ a photo of the statue.
7 _____ a newspaper.
8 _____ a sandwich.

b Write a letter in the box: A = plan, B = prediction.

1 I'm going to buy some souvenirs in the gift shop. ☐A
2 You're going to be hot in that jacket. ☐
3 My cousin is going to get married in the spring. ☐
4 We're going to be late if we don't hurry. ☐
5 There's going to be a beautiful sunset tonight. ☐
6 I think that factory's going to close. ☐
7 They're going to buy a new car. ☐
8 I'm going to book a holiday tomorrow. ☐

Study Link **Student's Book p.134** *Grammar Bank 7D*

3 PRONUNCIATION /ʊ/, /uː/, and /ʌ/

a Match the words to sounds 1, 2, and 3. Then connect the words that have the same sound.

1   2 [uː]   3 [ʌ]

1	good	student
	love	money
	music	cook

	hungry	book
	newspaper	lunch
	looking	true

b Practise saying the words.

c Complete the dialogues by using the pairs of matching words from exercise **a**.

1 Does your husband make the dinner?

  Yes, he's a very ___good___ ___cook___ .

2 What are the most important things in life?

  _____ and _____ .

3 What do you do?

  I'm a _____ _____ .

4 Can I help you?

  Yes, I'm _____ for a _____ about Italy.

5 A lot of the things you read in the _____ are

  often not _____ .

6 I'm _____ . What's for _____ ?

d Practise reading the dialogues.

More Words to Learn

Write translations and try to remember the words.

Word	Pronunciation	Translation
surprise *noun*	/səˈpraɪz/	
heart *noun*	/hɑːt/	
ring *noun*	/rɪŋ/	
(fifty-pound) note *noun*	/nəʊt/	
voice *noun*	/vɔɪs/	
card *noun*	/kɑːd/	
(I'm) sure *adjective*	/ʃʊə/	
put *verb*	/pʊt/	
maybe *adverb*	/ˈmeɪbi/	
soon *adverb*	/suːn/	

QUESTION TIME

Can you answer these questions?

1 What are you going to do this weekend?

2 Are you going to travel abroad this year?

3 Are you going to get married this year?

4 What are you going to have for dinner this evening?

5 Are you going to start a new job this year?

Study Link MultiROM

CAN YOU REMEMBER...?   FILES 6&7

Complete each space with one word.

1 There _____ any cupboards in the kitchen but there are some shelves.

2 _____ there many people at the football match last night?

3 Oh no! The baby _____ crying again.

4 She usually _____ trousers, but today she's wearing a skirt.

5 There's _____ milk in the fridge if you want it.

6 How _____ sandwiches do you want?

7 We're _____ to visit our cousins at the weekend.

8 When _____ you going to get married?

1 VOCABULARY AND READING

a Look at the menu and answer the questions.

1 Which is the best starter for somebody on a diet?
2 What main course can a vegetarian have?
3 Can you have fruit for dessert?
4 How many types of coffee are there?
5 Do children pay the same as adults?

Seaview Restaurant Menu

Starters

Soup of the day £3.50   Grilled low-fat goat's cheese (V) £3.95
Smoked salmon £5.95

Salads

Mixed salad (V) £5.50   Seafood salad £7.25

Main courses

Fillet steak, served with chips and carrots £10.75
Summer vegetable omelette (V) £6.95
Grilled tuna, served with a choice of fresh vegetables £9.95

Desserts

Cheesecake £2.95   Selection of ice cream £2.50
Cheese and biscuits £2.95

Beverages

Glass of wine (red or white) £1.95   Beer £2.25
Bottle of wine (red or white) £9.95   Soft drinks £1.75
Coffee (cappuccino or filter) £1.30

Set menu

£12.50 (see the board for today's choice)

25% discount on children's portions (V) vegetarian	Service charge is included

---

b Match the words and the definitions.

1 service charge   [f]
2 set menu   ☐
3 bookings   ☐
4 discount   ☐
5 beverages   ☐
6 soft drinks   ☐

a drinks
b reservations
c reduced price
d non-alcoholic drinks, e.g. Coke and lemonade
e a limited menu – you pay a fixed price and everything is included
f ~~extra money you pay for the waiters~~

c Underline five words or phrases you don't know. Use your dictionary to look up their meaning and pronunciation.

2 ORDERING A MEAL

Complete the dialogue with one word in each space.

A Good evening. Do you have a ¹ _reservation_ ?
B Yes, a ² _____ for two. My name's John McGeever.
A Smoking or ³ _____ ?
B Smoking, please.
A Come this way, please.

A Are you ready to ⁴ _____ ?
B Yes, ⁵ _____ like the mushroom risotto.
C Chicken salad ⁶ _____ me, please.
A What would you ⁷ _____ to drink?
B A glass of red wine and a mineral ⁸ _____ , please.

3 SOCIAL ENGLISH

Complete the dialogue with phrases a–e.

a Could we have the bill, please?
b ~~It was delicious.~~
c The same for me, please.
d Nothing for me, thanks.
e What is there?

A   Was the pasta good?
B   Yes, thanks. ¹ _b_
WAITER Would you like a dessert?
B   Yes, please. ² _____
WAITER Ice cream with chocolate sauce, or fruit salad.
B   The ice cream for me, please.
WAITER And you sir?
A   ³ _____
WAITER Here you are. Would you like any coffee?
B   Yes, a double espresso please.
A   ⁴ _____
WAITER Two double espressos. Anything else?
A   No, thank you. ⁵ _____

8 A The True False Show

Imagination is more important than knowledge.
Albert Einstein, German scientist

1 GRAMMAR comparative adjectives

a Write the comparative forms of these adjectives in the correct circle.

~~beautiful~~   dirty   cold   high   wet   cheap
good   dry   hungry   thin   sad   difficult
bad   comfortable   far

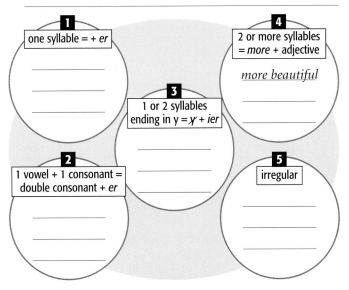

1 one syllable = + er

2 1 vowel + 1 consonant = double consonant + er

3 1 or 2 syllables ending in y = y + ier

4 2 or more syllables = more + adjective

more beautiful

5 irregular

b Write sentences using the opposite adjective.

1 A Fiat is **slower** than a Ferrari.

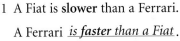
A Ferrari *is faster than a Fiat* .

2 The Pacific Ocean is **bigger** than the Atlantic Ocean.

The Atlantic Ocean _____ .

3 Germany is **wetter** than Tunisia.

Tunisia _____ .

4 The Suez Canal is **longer** than the Panama Canal.

The Panama Canal _____ .

5 Gold is **more expensive** than silver.

Silver _____ .

6 Olive oil is **better** for you than butter.

Butter _____ .

7 The sun is **hotter** than the moon.

The moon _____ .

8 English is **easier** than Chinese.

Chinese _____ .

> **Study Link** **Student's Book p.136** *Grammar Bank 8A*

2 PRONUNCIATION vowel sounds

a Write the words in the chart.

worse   slower   drier   ~~easier~~
healthier   dirtier   taller   better
colder   cheaper   higher   shorter

tree	horse	bird	egg	phone	bike
easier					

b Practise saying the words.

3 VOCABULARY personality adjectives

Complete the sentences with these words.

aggressive   stylish   generous   quiet
careful   ~~serious~~   friendly

1 Marc reads lots of books about politics. He's *serious* .

2 Maria likes buying people presents. She's _____ .

3 Caroline wears really nice clothes. She's _____ .

4 Jeanine loves going to parties and talking to people.

She's _____ .

5 Paolo argues a lot. He's _____ .

6 Lana plans things for a long time before she does them.

She's _____ .

7 Paul never says very much. He's _____ .

4 READING

a What do you think are the perfect colours to paint your flat or house? Look at the chart and complete column 1 (My opinion) with a colour from the box.

| blue | red/orange | green/white | yellow |

Rooms	1 My opinion	2 The expert's opinion
Bedroom		
Living room		
Dining room		
Study		

b Now read the text and complete column 2 (The expert's opinion). Do you agree?

Perfect colours, Perfect harmony

The colour you paint the rooms in your house can make you more comfortable. Follow the suggestions below to create the perfect atmosphere to eat, sleep, work, and relax in your own home.

The bedroom

The perfect colour for a bedroom is blue. It is a very relaxing colour, and can make you feel happier and more positive about life when you wake up in the morning.

The living room

The perfect colour for an elegant living room is green, with some white. Don't use dramatic colours like red, purple, and black because they don't help you relax.

The dining room

Red and orange are two colours which can make you feel hungrier at mealtimes. They also encourage more interesting conversation. But be careful! Only use these colours in small areas – a lot of red or orange can make you feel aggressive.

The study

Yellow is a beautiful colour which makes you feel happier and helps you to think, so it is a good colour for this room. It is also makes dark spaces a little brighter.

(adapted from a website)

c Look at the highlighted words. What do you think they mean? Check the ones you don't know in your dictionary.

d Read the text again. Mark the sentences T (True) or F (False).

1 A blue bedroom helps you to wake up earlier.   _F_

2 Green and white are dramatic colours.   ___

3 Red or orange in the dining room makes people eat and talk.   ___

4 A yellow study helps you to work better.   ___

More Words to Learn

Write translations and try to remember the words.

Word	Pronunciation	Translation
mo<u>squi</u>toes *noun*	/məˈskiːtəʊz/	
<u>sharks</u> *noun*	/ʃɑːks/	
<u>ti</u>gers *noun*	/ˈtaɪgəz/	
<u>a</u>dult *noun*	/ˈædʌlt/	
(make) jokes *noun*	/dʒəʊks/	
perso<u>na</u>lity *noun*	/pɜːsəˈnæləti/	
the Earth *noun*	/ðiː ɜːθ/	
Mars *noun*	/mɑːz/	

Study idea

Start a vocabulary notebook for new words you want to learn.

1 Write a translation, and use your dictionary to check the pronunciation.

2 Under<u>line</u> the stressed syllable.

Word	*Translation*
con<u>tes</u>tant	concursante

QUESTION TIME   ?

Can you answer these questions?

1 Is your country bigger or smaller than Britain?

2 Is it hotter or colder than Britain?

3 Is it wetter or drier than Britain?

4 Is it safer or more dangerous than Britain?

5 Is it cheaper or more expensive than Britain?

Study Link MultiROM

68

Study Link www.oup.com/elt/englishfile/elementary

8
B

The highest city in the world

The coldest winter I ever spent was a summer in San Francisco.

Mark Twain, American writer

1 GRAMMAR superlative adjectives

a Complete the chart.

adjective	comparative	superlative
cold	*colder*	*the coldest*
high		
expensive		
dry		
dangerous		
hot		
beautiful		
crowded		
good		
bad		

b Write the questions.

1 What / long river / world?

   What's the longest river in the world?

2 What / small country / world?

   _____

3 What / crowded country / world?

   _____

4 What / high mountain / world?

   _____

5 What / windy city / world?

   _____

6 What / small ocean / world?

   _____

7 What / expensive mineral / world?

   _____

8 What / dry place / world?

   _____

c Circle the correct answer to the questions in exercise **b**.

1 a (The Nile)   5 a Chicago, USA
  b The Danube   b La Paz, Bolivia
  c The Amazon   c Edinburgh, Scotland

2 a Andorra   6 a The Arctic Ocean
  b Monaco   b The Atlantic Ocean
  c The Vatican   c The Pacific Ocean

3 a India   7 a platinum
  b Bangladesh   b diamond
  c China   c graphite

4 a Mount Everest   8 a The Sahara Desert
  b Mont Blanc   b The Atacama Desert, Chile
  c Mount Kilimanjaro c The Arizona Desert, USA

d Write superlative sentences. Use the information in the chart.

Hotel	Size	Popular	Beautiful	Price
Minerva, Rome	24 rooms	☺☺☺	☺☺☺☺	€165 per night
Seine Palace, Paris	36 rooms	☺☺	☺☺☺	€190 per night
Victoria Inn, London	18 rooms	☺	☺☺	€210 per night
Rio Club, Rio de Janeiro	60 rooms	☺☺☺☺	☺☺☺	€130 per night

1 big   *The Rio Club is the biggest.*

2 small   _____.

3 popular   _____.

4 cheap   _____.

5 expensive _____.

6 beautiful _____.

Study Link **Student's Book p.136** *Grammar Bank 8B*

2 VOCABULARY the weather

Complete the sentences with a word from the box.

sunny	wet	~~hot~~	snowing	dry	cold
cloudy	windy				

1 It's _____hot_____.

2 It's _____.

3 It's _____.

4 It's _____.

5 It's _____.

6 It's _____.

7 It's _____.

8 It's _____.

3 PRONUNCIATION consonant groups

a Under<u>line</u> the stressed syllables.

1 the <u>most</u> <u>diff</u>icult   5 the coldest

2 the noisiest   6 the most crowded

3 the most expensive   7 the most beautiful

4 the fastest   8 the driest

b Practise saying the phrases.

More Words to Learn

Write translations and try to remember the words.

Word	Pronunciation	Translation
<u>o</u>xygen *noun*	/ˈɒksɪdʒən/	
beer *noun*	/bɪə/	
<u>air</u> con<u>di</u>tioning *noun*	/ˈeə kənˈdɪʃənɪŋ/	
<u>ca</u>pital *noun*	/ˈkæpɪtl/	
ge<u>o</u>graphy *noun*	/dʒiˈɒɡrəfi/	
<u>cli</u>mate *noun*	/ˈklaɪmət/	
<u>crow</u>ded *adjective*	/ˈkraʊdɪd/	
<u>bo</u>ring *adjective*	/ˈbɔːrɪŋ/	
i<u>ma</u>gine *verb*	/ɪˈmædʒɪn/	
sur<u>pri</u>singly *adverb*	/səˈpraɪzɪŋli/	

I'd like to live like a poor man, but with a lot of money.

Pablo Picasso, Spanish painter

Would you like to drive a Ferrari? WORKBOOK

1 GRAMMAR *would like to / like*

a Write the contractions.

1 He would like to see the film again.

He'd like to see the film again.

2 She would like to do a parachute jump.

_____ .

3 They would not like to go skiing.

_____ .

4 I would like to learn Chinese.

_____ .

5 We would not like to work in a fast-food restaurant.

_____ .

6 He would like to be lucky one day.

_____ .

7 You would not like to see that film.

_____ .

b Write sentences or questions with *would like.*
Use contractions.

1 he / be a teacher (–)

He wouldn't like to be a teacher.

2 you / be a ballet dancer (?)

_____ ?

3 we / live in a big city (+)

_____ .

4 I / learn how to fly a plane (+)

_____ .

5 she / work for that company (–)

_____ .

6 they / go to Chile on holiday (?)

_____ ?

c Choose the correct question.

1 **A** Do you like going for a walk?   ✗

   Would you like to go for a walk?   ✓

   B No, not now. I'm tired.

2 **A** Would you like a biscuit?

   Do you like a biscuit?

   B Yes, please. I'm quite hungry.

3 **A** Do you like your neighbours?

   Would you like your neighbours?

   B Yes, they're very friendly.

4 **A** What do you like doing tonight?

   What would you like to do tonight?

   B Let's go to the cinema.

5 **A** Would you like to go to the beach?

   Do you like going to the beach?

   B No, I don't. I don't like the sun.

d Circle the correct answer.

1 I'd like (to learn) / **learning** to dance salsa.

2 What does David like **do** / **doing** in his free time?

3 Do you like **cook** / **cooking**?

4 Would you like **to come** / **coming** to dinner tonight?

5 I wouldn't like **to go up** / **going up** in a hot air balloon.

6 I don't like **fly** / **flying**.

Study Link **Student's Book p.136** *Grammar Bank 8C*

71

2 PRONUNCIATION sentence stress

a Underline the stressed words.

1 A <u>Would</u> you like to drive a sports car?

   B Yes, I'd love to.

   A Why?

   B Because I love cars and I love driving.

2 A Would you like to ride a horse?

   B No, I wouldn't.

   A Why not?

   B Because I don't like horses.

b Practise saying the dialogues.

3 READING

a Read the text and write a letter in each space.

Which adventure experience...

1 ... can your family also enjoy? <u>B</u>

2 ... teaches you how to make your flat more comfortable? ___

3 ... helps you when you go to a restaurant? ___

4 ... gives you a free meal? ___

5 ... is not for people who don't like alcohol? ___

6 ... is not for people who can't swim? ___

b Look at the highlighted words. What do you think they mean? Check with your dictionary.

More Words to Learn

Write translations and try to remember the words.

Word	Pronunciation	Translation
dreams *noun*	/driːmz/	
weight *noun*	/weɪt/	
height *noun*	/haɪt/	
experience *noun*	/ɪkˈspɪəriəns/	
adventure *noun*	/ədˈventʃə/	
chef *noun*	/ʃef/	
jump *verb*	/dʒʌmp/	
last *verb*	/lɑːst/	
suddenly *adverb*	/ˈsʌdənli/	
including *preposition*	/ɪnˈkluːdɪŋ/	

Presents to remember

A Wine tasting

This is the perfect experience for stylish people who want to know the difference between a good wine and a bad wine. You can learn a lot

about wine and how it is made and you can try some excellent wines with the help of the experts. After this course you will know which wine to buy in the supermarket and which wine to order in a restaurant.

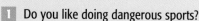

B Waterskiing

If you're a good swimmer, then why not try waterskiing? First you do a quick training course on land, and then you're ready to practise in the water. This activity is really exciting, and your friends and family can have a good time watching, too.

C Interior design tuition

If you want to change the style of your house, but you don't know where to start, then this is the present for you. Professional designers teach you how to use space, light, and colour. They also help you to be more creative by introducing your own personal style into your designs. Lunch is included in the course.

(adapted from a website)

1 GRAMMAR adverbs

a Complete the sentences with an adverb.

1 The Germans are careful drivers.

They drive ___carefully___.

2 The French cook perfect meals.

They cook _____.

3 The British are very polite.

They speak very _____.

4 The Brazilians are good at football.

They play football _____.

5 The Japanese are very hard workers.

They work very _____.

6 The Canadians eat healthy food.

They eat _____.

7 The Swedish speak beautiful English.

They speak English _____.

b Make adverbs from the adjectives and complete the sentences.

good   careful   hard
loud   stylish   ~~happy~~
generous   beautiful

The ideal partner...

1 ...does housework ___happily___.

2 ...dances _____.

3 ...cooks _____.

4 ...dresses _____.

5 ...drives _____.

6 ...gives presents _____.

7 ...works _____.

8 ...never speaks _____.

c Circle the correct answer.

1 My brother's a very (careful) / carefully driver.

2 Frank cooks very **good** / **well**.

3 Elena wears very **stylish** / **stylishly** clothes.

4 He always speaks very **aggressive** / **aggressively** to me.

5 He's very **quiet** / **quietly**. He never says anything!

6 She's **generous** / **generously**. She gives nice presents.

7 My French is very **bad** / **badly**.

8 Can you speak more **slow** / **slowly**?

Study Link **Student's Book p.136** *Grammar Bank 8D*

2 PRONUNCIATION adjectives and adverbs

a Under<u>line</u> the stressed syllables.

1 <u>bad</u>ly   4 politely   7 completely

2 dangerously   5 carefully   8 quietly

3 beautifully   6 slowly   9 stylishly

b Practise saying the words.

3 READING

a Read the story, and put the pictures in the correct order.

  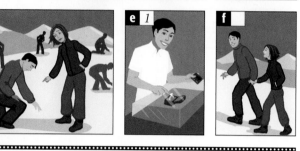

(adapted from a website)

Romance…without a ring!

A couple from Colorado USA had a big surprise last Saturday when they lost a $4,000 ring at the top of a mountain.

Derek Monnig, 33, bought the diamond ring for his girlfriend, Debra Sweeney, 34, to celebrate their engagement. He wanted to ask her to marry him in a very romantic place, so they walked slowly in the snow to the top of the Rocky Mountains. They stopped and Derek said, 'I have something for you. Honey, I love you. Will you marry me?'

Suddenly, he took the ring out of his pocket and started to put it on her finger. But the ring fell into the snow near Debra's boot. They started to look for it, and other people came quickly to help them, but they couldn't find it, so they called the ski patrol. Seven more men came to help. They spent two hours with them trying to find the ring. The next day the couple went back to the mountain with a metal detector, but they never found it.

Debra wasn't too unhappy. 'It's much better to lose the ring than the guy,' she said. And luckily the ring was insured.

b Write T (True) or F (False).

1 Derek and Debra wanted to get married on top of a mountain.   _F_

2 Derek had the ring in his pocket.   ___

3 The ring fell into Debra's boot.   ___

4 Seven people helped them look for the ring.   ___

5 They spent all day looking for the ring.   ___

6 The couple went back again with a metal detector.   ___

c Guess the meaning of the highlighted words. Then check with your dictionary.

More Words to Learn

Write translations and try to remember the words.

Word	Pronunciation	Translation
social life *noun*	/'səʊʃl laɪf/	
crime *noun*	/kraɪm/	
shy *adjective*	/ʃaɪ/	
polite *adjective*	/pə'laɪt/	
elegant *adjective*	/'elɪgənt/	
steal *verb*	/stiːl/	
dress *verb*	/dres/	
everywhere *adverb*	/'evriweə/	
abroad *adverb*	/ə'brɔːd/	
almost *adverb*	/'ɔːlməʊst/	

QUESTION TIME ?

Can you answer these questions?

1 Do you speak English well or badly?
2 Do you eat healthily or unhealthily?
3 Do you drive fast or slowly?
4 Do you speak quietly or loudly?
5 Do you play any sport very well?

Study Link MultiROM

CAN YOU REMEMBER…? FILES 7&8

Complete each space with one word.

1 Is there _____ sugar in this coffee?
2 How _____ money do you have with you?
3 Who are you _____ to go on holiday with?
4 I think _____ going to rain.
5 His office is bigger _____ mine.
6 Who's _____ tallest person in your family?
7 I _____ like to do a parachute jump. I don't like flying.
8 My father drives very _____. He never goes at more than 80 kph.

1 VOCABULARY verb phrases

Match the phrases.

1 I'd like to   [b]   a a taxi?
2 Could I have   ☐   b ~~check out.~~
3 Can I pay   ☐   c help with your luggage?
4 Please sign   ☐   d by credit card?
5 Do you need any   ☐   e your name here.
6 Can you call me   ☐   f the bill, please?

2 CHECKING OUT

Order the dialogue.

B Of course. ☐
B Room 223. ☐
A Yes. Which room is it? ☐
B No, but I had a beer from the minibar last night. ☐
A Thank you very much. Have a good trip. ☐
A Good morning, madam. [1]
B Morning. Can I have the bill, please? [2]
A Right, can you sign here, please? ☐
A Did you make any phone calls? ☐
B Thank you. Goodbye. ☐

3 SOCIAL ENGLISH

Complete the spaces with a phrase from the box.

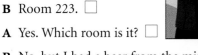

| a good trip | can we meet | ~~I'll call~~ |
| I'll meet you | I'll e-mail you | I'm late |

A Oh no, I'm going to be late for my train.
B Don't worry. [1] _____I'll call_____ a taxi.

A [2]_____ at the airport.
B OK. Where [3]_____ ?
A At the information desk, at 7 o'clock.

A Sorry [4]_____ .
B No problem. We have time.

A Have [5]_____ . And please write.
B [6]_____ next week, I promise.

4 READING

a Read the text about Glasgow airport.

GLASGOW AIRPORT

Glasgow Airport is the busiest of Scotland's three main international airports, and 7.5 million passengers pass through it every year. Below you can find five different ways of getting to the airport:

➤ BY CAR
If you're planning to drive to Glasgow Airport, you need to take the M8 motorway and turn off at junction 28. The airport is a 20-minute drive from Glasgow city centre and two minutes from the nearest town, Paisley.

➤ BY BIKE
The National Cycle Network Route will take you to the airport, where there is a safe place you can keep your bike until you need it again when you return. Take National Routes 75 and 7 to ride through Paisley to Glasgow Airport.

➤ BY TRAIN
The train will take you from Glasgow Central to Paisley's Gilmour Street Station, where you can take a taxi or a bus for the remaining three kilometres to Glasgow Airport. From Monday to Saturday there are eight trains an hour, and there are five every hour on a Sunday.

➤ BY BUS OR COACH
Citylink and Fairline buses operate a service to the airport from Glasgow city centre. The buses run every 15 minutes and drop you off in front of the terminal building. The price for a single ticket is £3.30, and the journey takes about 25 minutes.

➤ BY TAXI
Phone Cab Fly 24 hours a day on +44 (0)141 848 4588 for a taxi to take you to Glasgow Airport. The cost of a taxi from Glasgow city centre to the airport is approximately £16.50, and the journey takes about 20 minutes.

(adapted from a website)

b How did the following people get to the airport?

1 James went on the motorway.   _____by car_____
2 Sarah paid £3.30.   _____
3 Robert made a phone call.   _____
4 Steve did some exercise.   _____
5 Carol went from Glasgow Central.   _____

c <u>Underline</u> five words or phrases you don't know. Use your dictionary to look up their meaning and pronunciation.

O beware my lord of jealousy! It is the green-eyed monster…
William Shakespeare, English dramatist

9A Before we met

1 VOCABULARY 'jealous' reading

Complete the sentences with these words.

holiday brochure   ~~reply~~   silence
fun   pick up

1 I asked him a question, but he didn't
   _____*reply*_____ .

2 **A** How did you find this hotel?
   B I saw it in a _____ .

3 I like walking in the mountains – I love
   the _____ .

4 Could you _____ those sweet papers?

5 **A** Did you have a good time at the party
   last night?
   B Yes, it was _____ .

2 GRAMMAR present perfect

a Write the contractions.

1 I have not been to Thailand.
   I haven't been to Thailand.

2 Tim has not been to a Japanese restaurant.
   _____

3 We have been to this city before.
   _____

4 I have been to this bar lots of times.
   _____

5 They have not been to New York.
   _____

6 My girlfriend has been to Paris twice.
   _____

7 He has been to Brazil.
   _____

8 We have not been to Mexico.
   _____

b Write sentences.

1 Brazil   *She's been to Brazil.*
2 Australia   *They've been to Australia.*
3 Japan   _____ .
4 Thailand   _____ .
5 Canada   _____ .
6 China   _____ .
7 Malaysia   _____ .
8 Argentina   _____ .

c Complete the dialogue.

A Have you [1] _____*been*_____ to the USA?
B No, I [2] _____ , but my wife has.
A Where [3] _____ she been to in the USA?
B Only New York.
A Has she [4] _____ to Canada?
B No, she [5] _____ . But we'd like to go there for a holiday.
A And [6] _____ you been to Australia?
B No, I [7] _____ . Have you?
A Yes, I [8] _____ . I've been to Sydney and Canberra.

Study Link **Student's Book p.138** *Grammar Bank 9A*

3 VOCABULARY town and city

Where have these people been? Complete the sentences.

1 She's been to the
   market .

2 He's been to the
   b_____ .

3 They've been to the
   t_____ .

4 He's been to the
   s_____ .

5 She's been to the
   h_____ .

6 He's been to the
   s_____ c_____ .

7 She's been to the
   c_____ .

8 They've been to the
   t_____ a_____ .

Study Link **Student's Book p.152** *Vocabulary Bank*

4 PRONUNCIATION

Circle the word with a different sound. Practise saying the words.

ɒ	opera	want	concert	(country)
3ː	Thursday	really	girlfriend	person
e	jealous	never	break	tell
k	cinema	continent	karaoke	pick up
dʒ	June	Germany	travel agent	angry
h	have	holiday	hour	hotel

More Words to Learn

Write translations and try to remember the words.

Word	Pronunciation	Translation
sports event *noun*	/ˈspɔːts ɪˈvent/	
continent *noun*	/ˈkɒntɪnənt/	
spa *noun*	/spɑː/	
miles *noun*	/maɪlz/	
jealous *adjective*	/ˈdʒeləs/	
ring *verb*	/rɪŋ/	
exactly *adverb*	/ɪgˈzæktli/	
somewhere *adverb*	/ˈsʌmweə/	

Study idea

Look back at the eight **Study ideas** in this workbook. Which ones do you do?

QUESTION TIME

Can you answer these questions?

1 Have you been to work today?
2 Have you been to the supermarket today?
3 Have you been to a restaurant today?
4 Have you been to the cinema today?
5 Have you been to a friend's house today?

Study Link MultiROM

Study Link www.oup.com/elt/englishfile/elementary

Films should have a beginning, a middle, and an end – but not necessarily in that order.

Jean-Luc Godard, French film director

I've read the book, I've seen the film

1 VOCABULARY past participles

a Write the past participles of these irregular verbs.

infinitive	past simple	past participle
break	broke	*broken*
buy	bought	
drive	drove	
find	found	
give	gave	
lose	lost	
make	made	
run	ran	
write	wrote	

b Use past participles from the chart to complete the sentences.

1 Debbie and Fernando have ___*bought*___ a new house.

2 I've never _____ a marathon.

3 Daniel has _____ his girlfriend some flowers.

4 John Grisham has _____ many bestsellers.

5 Have you ever _____ your leg?

6 I'm going to be late. I've _____ the car keys.

7 You've _____ a lot of mistakes.

8 She _____ some money in the street.

9 I've never _____ a Ferrari.

2 PRONUNCIATION irregular participles

Circle the word with a different vowel sound.
Practise saying the words.

🐟	🦀	🥚 e	⬆ ʌ	🎂 eɪ	☎ əʊ
given	found	left	come	taken	known
written	thought	heard	done	made	lost
(seen)	caught	said	drunk	read	broken
driven	worn	sent	got	paid	spoken

3 GRAMMAR present perfect or past simple?

a Circle the correct form.

1 I (didn't meet)/ have never met anyone nice at the party.

2 Miko went / has been to the cinema last weekend.

3 Did you read / Have you read any books by John Irving?

4 Lucy's a journalist. She met / has met a lot of interesting people.

5 They started / have started to watch the film, but they fell asleep before the end.

6 We didn't see / haven't seen the film yesterday because the cinema was full.

7 I didn't read / haven't read any Terry Pratchett books. I don't like science fiction.

8 Did you go / Have you been to that new restaurant in the city centre last Saturday?

b Complete the dialogues with the correct form of the verbs in brackets.

A ¹ *Have you read* (read) any of the Harry Potter books?

B Yes, I have. My brother ² _____ (give) them to me for my last birthday.

A Which one ³ _____ you _____ (like) best?

B The first one. I ⁴ _____ (read) it five times.

A ⁵ _____ you _____ (see) the new Almodóvar film?

B Yes, I have. I ⁶ _____ (take) my boyfriend to see it last night.

A ⁷ _____ (be) it good?

B No, I ⁸ _____ _____ (not / enjoy) it.

Study Link **Student's Book p.138** *Grammar Bank 9B*

4 READING

The richest woman in Britain

The richest woman in the UK is now Joanne Kathleen Rowling, the author of the Harry Potter books. But life hasn't always been easy for her.

She was born on 31st July 1965 and started writing at the early age of six. At school she was very quiet and didn't like sport much. Her favourite subjects were English and Modern Languages. After school she studied French at Exeter University and she later became a bilingual secretary. She didn't enjoy her life as a secretary and when she was 26 she left the UK to teach English in Portugal. She met and married a journalist and their daughter, Jessica, was born in 1993. The marriage ended in divorce and Ms Rowling moved to Edinburgh, Scotland. It was during this period that she started her first Harry Potter novel, which she wrote in a café while her daughter was asleep.

She published *Harry Potter and the Philosopher's Stone* in 1997 and in the same year she won one of the most important book awards in Britain. Since then millions of people have read her books in many different languages, and millions have seen the Harry Potter films. Everybody knows who she is and everybody has heard of the famous character she has created. Harry Potter is possibly the most famous boy in the world.

(adapted from a website)

Read the text and answer the questions.

1   When was J K Rowling born?

2   How old was she when she started writing?

3   What were her favourite subjects at school?

4   What two jobs did she do before she became a writer?

5   Why did she go to Portugal?

6   What does her ex-husband do?

7   When was her daughter born?

8   Where did she write the first Harry Potter novel?

9   When did she win a book award?

10 How many people have read her books and seen the films?

More Words to Learn

Write translations and try to remember the words.

Word	Pronunciation	Translation
back <u>row</u> *noun*	/bæk ˈrəʊ/	
<u>sound</u>track *noun*	/ˈsaʊndtræk/	
<u>au</u>tograph *noun*	/ˈɔːtəɡrɑːf/	
best<u>sel</u>ler *noun*	/bestˈselə/	
<u>ver</u>sion *noun*	/vɜːʒn/	
pre<u>fer</u> *verb*	/prɪˈfɜː/	
<u>based</u> on	/beɪst ɒn/	

QUESTION TIME

Can you answer these questions?

1   Have you ever cried in a film?

2   Have you ever spoken to an actor?

3   Have you ever slept in the cinema?

4   Have you ever seen a film more than three times?

5   Have you ever left a film early?

Study Link MultiROM

CAN YOU REMEMBER...? FILES 8&9

Complete each space with one word.

1   A lot of people like rock music – it's _____ popular than classical music.

2   _____ you like to go up in a hot-air balloon?

3   Siberia is the _____ place in the world.

4   Your English is good. You speak very _____ .

5   I've never _____ to the UK.

6   _____ you ever driven a Ferrari?

1 GRAMMAR

a 1 was 2 was 3 Was 4 wasn't
  5 was 6 was 7 was 8 was
  9 was 10 were

b 1 Was Mozart from Germany? No, he
    wasn't.
  2 Were Columbus and Magellan
    explorers? Yes, they were.
  3 Was Virginia Woolf a writer? Yes, she
    was.
  4 Were the Bee Gees from the USA?
    No, they weren't.
  5 Was John McEnroe a footballer? No,
    he wasn't.
  6 Was Matisse a composer? No, he
    wasn't.
  7 Was Picasso born in Spain? Yes, he
    was.
  8 Was Greta Garbo an actress? Yes, she
    was.
  9 Were Tolstoy and Cervantes
    painters? No, they weren't.
  10 Was Nelson Mandela born in
    Britain? No, he wasn't.

c 1 is, was 2 Is, isn't, was, is
  3 were, are 4 was, were 5 was, was

2 VOCABULARY

a/b 1 an inventor 2 a writer
  3 a politician 4 a composer
  5 a musician 6 a painter 7 a leader
  8 an actor 9 a scientist 10 a sailor

d 1 was a scientist   6 were writers
  2 were inventors   7 was a politician
  3 was a painter   8 was a sailor
  4 was a composer   9 were actors
  5 was a musician

1 PRONUNCIATION

a 1 wanted 2 painted 3 waited
  4 landed 5 started 6 decided

2 GRAMMAR

a 1 walked, didn't walk
  2 studied, didn't study
  3 helped, didn't help
  4 played, didn't play
  5 booked, didn't book
  6 painted, didn't paint
  7 worked, didn't work
  8 showed, didn't show

b 1 Was Peter tired after the match?
  2 Where were you last night?
  3 Were they late for the concert?
  4 Where did they land the plane?
  5 What university did your brother
    study at?
  6 Was your first boyfriend very tall?
  7 Why didn't you wait for the bus?
  8 What time did Sandra arrive at work
    yesterday?

c 1 When did the Wall Street crash
    happen? 1929
  2 When did the Second World War
    finish? 1945
  3 When did Neil Armstrong land on
    the moon? 1969
  4 When did mobile phones first
    appear? 1985
  5 When did John Logie Baird invent
    the television? 1925
  6 When did George Harrison die?
    2001
  7 When did Bill Gates start Microsoft?
    1975

3 VOCABULARY

1 last night 2 two years ago
3 last month 4 yesterday morning
5 two hours ago 6 last July
7 two weeks ago 8 yesterday afternoon

1 VOCABULARY

a 1 a bus 2 for a walk 3 a good time
  4 a taxi 5 18 years 6 shopping

b 1 went 2 got 3 had 4 went
  5 got 6 had 7 got 8 went
  9 had 10 went 11 had 12 had

2 GRAMMAR

a 1 Robert wore a tie to work yesterday.
  2 They did their homework together
    last night.
  3 Helen didn't go to the shops last
    week.
  4 We met in the bar last night.
  5 We didn't have dinner at home last
    night.
  6 Jane got up early yesterday morning.
  7 He bought a newspaper at the
    station yesterday.
  8 I left home at 7.00 yesterday.
  9 She saw her friends after work last
    night.
  10 Bob couldn't come to dinner last
    week.

b 1 did you go 2 Was it 3 did you go
  4 did you wear 5 did you get
  6 Did you get 7 you have 8 Was

3 READING

b 1 F 2 F 3 T 4 T 5 T 6 T
  7 F 8 T

4 PRONUNCIATION

a /æ/ came /ɒ/ wrote /ɔː/ heard
  /eɪ/ said /e/ knew

1 PRONUNCIATION

a 1 made 2 said 3 lost 4 had
  5 bought 6 drove 7 could
  8 learnt

2 VOCABULARY

a **Infinitive:** begin, come, drink, drive,
  give, know, put, ring, sit, wake, win,
  write
  Past: began, came, drank, drove, gave,
  knew, put, rang, sat, woke, won, wrote

b 1 got, heard 2 met 3 bought
  4 went 5 made 6 didn't take
  7 found 8 lost 9 thought
  10 couldn't

3 GRAMMAR

a 1 arrived 2 left 3 was 4 were
  5 looked 6 saw 7 couldn't
  8 opened 9 didn't run 10 went
  11 found 12 didn't want 13 took

b 1 were you   6 did you do
  2 did you see   7 did you leave
  3 did you go   8 Did you go
  4 Did she like   9 Did you get
  5 did ... finish   10 did you go

CAN YOU REMEMBER?

1 Can 2 going 3 us 4 ours
5 were 6 didn't 7 have 8 went

PRACTICAL ENGLISH 5

1 VOCABULARY

1 postcards 2 film 3 mug
4 T-shirts 5 batteries

2 BUYING A PRESENT

Next, please 1
No, thanks. Just the mug. 12
It's five pounds. 7
How much is a large mug? 6
These mugs are quite cheap. 5
How much are the T-shirts? 2
Red, please. 10
Red or blue? 9
Oh! They're very expensive! 4
Here you are. Anything else? 11
They're 30 pounds. 3
OK. Can I have a mug, please? 8

3 SOCIAL ENGLISH

1 Wow 2 look 3 nice 4 believe
5 problem 6 Come 7 time 8 Relax

4 READING

a 1 shops 2 cup 3 biscuits
  4 popular 5 find 6 love

6A WORKBOOK KEY

1 VOCABULARY

a 1 hall 2 bathroom 3 dining room
  4 study 5 garage 6 kitchen
  7 living room 8 bedroom

b **Across:** 1 cupboard, 3 carpet, 7 mirror,
  8 sofa, 9 cooker, 10 bed, 11 lamp,
  12 fireplace
  Down: 2 picture, 4 fridge, 5 stairs,
  6 armchair, 10 bath

2 GRAMMAR

a 1 Is there a 2 there's a 3 are there
  4 there are 5 is there a 6 there isn't
  7 there's a 8 Are there any
  9 there aren't 10 there are some
  11 are there any 12 There aren't any
  13 there's a

b 1 There are some cigarettes on the floor.
  2 Are there any plants in your living
    room?
  3 There are some keys in that door.
  4 Are there any toilets in this
    restaurant?
  5 There aren't any windows in this
    room.

c 1 It's 2 There's 3 there are
  4 they are 5 There's 6 there aren't
  7 there are 8 They are 9 it isn't
  10 there's

3 PRONUNCIATION

a /ð/ think /θ/ that /eə/ here
  /ɪə/ wear

b 1 carpet 2 mirror 3 cupboard
  4 fantastic 5 cooker 6 sofa
  7 armchair 8 information

6B WORKBOOK KEY

1 VOCABULARY

1 in 2 next to 3 under
4 in front of 5 opposite 6 behind
7 in 8 on 9 over 10 between

2 GRAMMAR

a 1 were 2 was 3 weren't 4 were
  5 wasn't 6 were 7 was 8 was
  9 weren't

b 1 Was there   7 there weren't
  2 there were   8 there were
  3 There was   9 Was there
  4 there wasn't   10 there wasn't
  5 There was   11 there were
  6 Were there

---

3 READING

b 1 approximately 400 years old
  2 the owners 3 swim, sunbathe
  4 ten 5 in the dining area outside
  6 twice a week

4 PRONUNCIATION

a 1 g̶host 2 autum̶n 3 com̶b
  4 listen 5 w̶hite 6 coul̶d 7 w̶rite
  8 hal̶f 9 cup̶board 10 h̶our

6C WORKBOOK KEY

1 VOCABULARY

1 argue 2 barks 3 cries 4 plays
5 talk 6 move 7 watch 8 have

2 GRAMMAR

a 1 are you doing
  2 'm looking
  3 are they doing
  4 Is Mrs Jackson watching
  5 's moving
  6 is Mr Jackson playing
  7 are arriving
  8 is opening

b 1 The dog's barking.
  2 The baby's crying.
  3 The boy and girl are arguing.
  4 The woman is taking her dog for a
    walk.
  5 The boys are playing football.
  6 The man is eating a sandwich.
  7 The two women are running.
  8 The old man is reading a newspaper.

3 PRONUNCIATION

a /ɪ/ writing /iː/ hearing /ɔː/ working
  /eɪ/ having /əʊ/ doing /aɪ/ living

4 READING

b 2, 3, 5, 6

6 D — WORKBOOK KEY

1 GRAMMAR

a 1 What are you doing   2 Do you walk
  3 's buying   4 'm going   5 rains
  6 's talking   7 Does your baby cry
  8 watches

b 1 does he start   2 's having
  3 's doing   4 don't like   5 are looking
  6 cooks   7 'm watching   8 goes
  9 don't want   10 are you going

2 VOCABULARY

a 1 art gallery   2 shopping centre
  3 railway station   4 travel agent's
  5 police station   6 department store
  7 sports centre

b 1 school   2 church   3 hospital
  4 museum   5 bridge   6 mosque
  7 castle   8 square   9 park
  10 chemist's   11 theatre

3 PRONUNCIATION

a 1 cen<u>t</u>re   2 show<u>er</u>   3 opp<u>o</u>site
  4 sof<u>a</u>   5 pic<u>t</u>ure   6 <u>a</u>go   7 thea<u>tre</u>
  8 mir<u>r</u>or   9 <u>t</u>omorrow   10 par<u>e</u>nt

CAN YOU REMEMBER?

1 were   2 Did   3 had   4 didn't
5 are   6 weren't   7 making   8 Are

PRACTICAL ENGLISH 6

1 VOCABULARY

1 corner   2 traffic lights
3 roundabout   4 opposite   5 left
6 right   7 straight on   8 past

2 ASKING FOR DIRECTIONS

1 Excuse   2 Where's   3 near
4 exactly   5 tell   6 way   7 first
8 say

3 SOCIAL ENGLISH

1 b   2 c   3 d   4 a

4 READING

b 1 the tube
  2 in the rush hour
  3 upstairs on a bus
  4 on buses and the underground
  5 they're expensive
  6 £5

c very big – enormous
  very good – excellent
  quite cheap – economical
  full of people – crowded
  difficult to understand – confusing

7 A — WORKBOOK KEY

1 VOCABULARY

a **Across:** 2 cereal, 4 fish, 6 oranges,
  7 pasta, 8 eggs, 10 apple, 11 meat,
  12 bread
  Down: 1 peas, 2 cheese, 3 lettuce,
  5 potatoes, 9 salad

b **Vegetables:** carrots, onions,
  mushrooms, peas
  Snacks: cake, crisps, chocolate, biscuits
  Fruit: apples, pineapple, grapes,
  bananas

2 GRAMMAR

a 1 some   2 an   3 some   4 some
  5 some   6 a   7 a   8 some   9 an
  10 some

b 1 There isn't any rice in the cupboard.
  2 ate some fruit yesterday
  3 had an egg for breakfast
  4 is some sugar in this coffee
  5 don't have any vegetables in the
    garden
  6 were some sandwiches in the fridge
  7 wasn't any nice fish at the
    supermarket
  8 didn't have a salad for lunch

c 1 some   2 a   3 some   4 some
  5 any   6 a   7 some   8 some   9 an
  10 any   11 some

3 PRONUNCIATION

/iː/ breakfast   /e/ ice cream   /eɪ/ eat

4 READING

a A 3, B 2, C 4, D 1

7 B — WORKBOOK KEY

1 PRONUNCIATION

a **William:** wine, wallet, watch, walkman
  Vera: video recorder, vase, vodka
  Brenda: boots, bird, book, bike

2 GRAMMAR

a 1 How many cigarettes do you smoke?
    He doesn't smoke many cigarettes.
  2 How much fruit do you eat?
    He eats a lot of fruit.
  3 How much milk do you drink?
    She drinks quite a lot of milk.
  4 How much exercise do you do?
    He doesn't do much exercise.
  5 How many cups of tea do you drink?
    She doesn't drink any (cups of) tea.
  6 How many biscuits do you eat?
    She doesn't eat many biscuits.

b 1 How many hamburgers did Nikolai
    Cohen eat?
  2 How much milk did Gustav Sajer
    drink?
  3 How much ice cream did John
    Edwards eat?
  4 How many chicken wings did
    George Willis eat?
  5 How much fruit did Barbara Beard
    eat?
  6 How many hot dogs did Alina Baden
    eat?

3 VOCABULARY

1 beer   2 wine   3 orange juice
4 milk   5 mineral water   6 coffee
7 tea   8 Coke

4 VOCABULARY

1 sweat   2 In fact   3 temperature
4 experiments   5 contain   6 at least
7 myth

7 C — WORKBOOK KEY

1 GRAMMAR

a 1 She's going to enjoy the holiday.
  2 We aren't going to stay in a hotel.
  3 They're going to go swimming.
  4 I'm going to go camping.
  5 Are you going to pay for the trip?
  6 He isn't going to see the pyramids.

b 1 are they going to leave
  2 're going to try
  3 're going to have
  4 Are you going to stay
  5 're not going to get married
  6 Are they going to see
  7 's going to meet
  8 isn't going to go

c 1 are you going to go
  2 're going to travel
  3 are you going to visit
  4 are you going to sleep
  5 aren't going to stay
  6 's going to be
  7 are you going to go
  8 're going to get
  9 's going to come
  10 'm going to go
  11 'm going to spend
  12 'm not going to get

2 PRONUNCIATION

a 1 <u>ho</u>liday   2 <u>ho</u>tel   3 <u>cam</u>psite
  4 <u>wea</u>ther   5 mu<u>se</u>um   6 <u>res</u>taurant
  7 <u>night</u>life   8 <u>pro</u>gramme

3 VOCABULARY

stay: in a hotel, at a campsite, in a bed and breakfast

go: on holiday, shopping, to the beach

see: the sights, a show, the Statue of Liberty

4 READING

b 1 C 2 B 3 A 4 D

c 1 penguin 2 turtle 3 elephant
   4 earth 5 hot-air balloon 6 spaceship

 7 D

WORKBOOK KEY

1 VOCABULARY

1 be 2 have 3 get / be 4 be
5 fall / be 6 move 7 have 8 move
9 get / have 10 meet 11 have

2 GRAMMAR

a 1 She's going to eat
  2 He's going to fall
  3 She's going to get
  4 He's going to have
  5 They're going to see
  6 He's going to take
  7 She's going to buy
  8 He's going to make

b 1 A 2 B 3 A 4 B 5 B 6 B
  7 A 8 A

3 PRONUNCIATION

a 1 good / cook, 2 music / student,
  3 love / money
  1 looking / book, 2 newspaper / true,
  3 hungry / lunch

c 1 good cook   4 looking, book
  2 Love, money   5 newspaper, true
  3 music student 6 hungry, lunch

CAN YOU REMEMBER?

1 aren't 2 Were 3 is 4 wears
5 some 6 many 7 going 8 are

PRACTICAL ENGLISH 7

1 VOCABULARY AND READING

a 1 Grilled low-fat goat's cheese
  2 Summer vegetable omelette
  3 no 4 two 5 no

b 1 f 2 e 3 b 4 c 5 a 6 d

2 ORDERING A MEAL

1 reservation 2 table 3 non-smoking
4 order 5 I'd 6 for 7 like 8 water

3 SOCIAL ENGLISH

1 b 2 e 3 d 4 c 5 a

 8 A

WORKBOOK KEY

1 GRAMMAR

a 1 colder, higher, cheaper
  2 wetter, thinner, sadder
  3 dirtier, drier, hungrier
  4 more beautiful, more difficult, more comfortable
  5 better, worse, further

b 1 is faster than a Fiat
  2 is smaller than the Pacific Ocean
  3 is drier than Germany
  4 is shorter than the Suez Canal
  5 is cheaper than gold
  6 is worse for you than olive oil
  7 is colder than the sun
  8 is more difficult than English

2 PRONUNCIATION

a /iː/ easier, cheaper /e/ healthier, better
  /ɔː/ taller, shorter /əʊ/ slower, colder
  /ɜː/ worse, dirtier /aɪ/ drier, higher

3 VOCABULARY

1 serious 2 generous 3 stylish
4 friendly 5 aggressive 6 careful
7 quiet

4 READING

b blue, green/white, red/orange, yellow

d 1 F 2 F 3 T 4 T

 8 B

WORKBOOK KEY

1 GRAMMAR

a **Comparative:** colder, higher, more expensive, drier, more dangerous, hotter, more beautiful, more crowded, better, worse
  Superlative: the coldest, the highest, the most expensive, the driest, the most dangerous, the hottest, the most beautiful, the most crowded, the best, the worst

b 1 What's the longest river in the world?
  2 What's the smallest country in the world?
  3 What's the most crowded country in the world?
  4 What's the highest mountain in the world?
  5 What's the windiest city in the world?
  6 What's the smallest ocean in the world?
  7 What's the most expensive mineral in the world?
  8 What's the driest place in the world?

c 1 a 2 c 3 b 4 a 5 a 6 a
  7 a 8 b

d 1 The Rio Club is the biggest.
  2 The Victoria Inn is the smallest.
  3 The Rio Club is the most popular.
  4 The Rio Club is the cheapest.
  5 The Victoria Inn is the most expensive.
  6 The Minerva is the most beautiful.

2 VOCABULARY

1 hot 2 cold 3 dry 4 wet 5 snowing
6 windy 7 sunny 8 cloudy

3 PRONUNCIATION

a 1 the <u>most</u> difficult
  2 the <u>noisiest</u>
  3 the <u>most</u> expensive
  4 the <u>fastest</u>
  5 the <u>coldest</u>
  6 the <u>most</u> crowded
  7 the <u>most</u> beautiful
  8 the <u>driest</u>

8 C

WORKBOOK KEY

1 GRAMMAR

a 1 He'd like to see the film again.
  2 She'd like to do a parachute jump.
  3 They wouldn't like to go skiing.
  4 I'd like to learn Chinese.
  5 We wouldn't like to work in a fast-food restaurant.
  6 He'd like to be lucky one day.
  7 You wouldn't like to see that film.

b 1 He wouldn't like to be a teacher.
  2 Would you like to be a ballet dancer?
  3 We'd like to live in a big city.
  4 I'd like to learn how to fly a plane.
  5 She wouldn't like to work for that company.
  6 Would they like to go to Chile on holiday?

c 1 Would you like to go for a walk?
  2 Would you like a biscuit?
  3 Do you like your neighbours?
  4 What would you like to do tonight?
  5 Do you like going to the beach?

d 1 to learn 2 doing 3 cooking
  4 to come 5 to go up 6 flying

2 PRONUNCIATION

a 1 A <u>Would</u> you <u>like</u> to <u>drive</u> a <u>sports</u> car?
    B <u>Yes</u>, I'd <u>love</u> to.
    A Why?
    B Because I <u>love</u> <u>cars</u> and <u>driving</u>.
  2 A <u>Would</u> you <u>like</u> to <u>ride</u> a <u>horse</u>?
    B <u>No</u>, I <u>wouldn't</u>.
    A Why <u>not</u>?
    B Because I <u>don't</u> <u>like</u> horses.

3 READING

a 1 B 2 C 3 A 4 C 5 A 6 B

1 GRAMMAR

a 1 carefully 2 perfectly 3 politely
  4 well 5 hard 6 healthily
  7 beautifully

b 1 happily 2 beautifully / well 3 well
  4 stylishly / well 5 carefully / well
  6 generously 7 hard 8 loudly

c 1 careful 2 well 3 stylish
  4 aggressively 5 quiet 6 generous
  7 bad 8 slowly

2 PRONUNCIATION

a 1 <u>bad</u>ly 2 <u>dan</u>gerously 3 <u>beau</u>tifully
  4 po<u>lite</u>ly 5 <u>care</u>fully 6 <u>slow</u>ly
  7 com<u>plete</u>ly 8 <u>qui</u>etly 9 <u>sty</u>lishly

3 READING

a a 3 b 6 c 4 d 5 e 1 f 2

b 1 F 2 T 3 F 4 F 5 F 6 T

CAN YOU REMEMBER?

1 any 2 much 3 going 4 it's
5 than 6 the 7 wouldn't 8 slowly

PRACTICAL ENGLISH 8

1 VOCABULARY

1 b 2 f 3 d 4 e 5 c 6 a

2 CHECKING OUT

Of course. 8
Room 223. 4
Yes. Which room is it? 3
No, but I had a beer … 6
Thank you very much. Have … 9
Good morning, madam. 1
Morning. Can I have the bill, please? 2
Right, can you sign here, please? 7
Did you make any phone calls? 5
Thank you. Goodbye. 10

3 SOCIAL ENGLISH

1 I'll call   4 I'm late
2 I'll meet you   5 a good trip
3 can we meet   6 I'll e-mail you

4 READING

b 1 by car 2 by bus 3 by taxi
  4 by bike 5 by train

---

1 VOCABULARY

1 reply 2 holiday brochure 3 silence
4 pick up 5 fun

2 GRAMMAR

a 1 I haven't been to Thailand.
  2 Tim hasn't been to a Japanese restaurant.
  3 We've been to this city before.
  4 I've been to this bar lots of times.
  5 They haven't been to New York.
  6 My girlfriend's been to Paris twice.
  7 He's been to Brazil.
  8 We haven't been to Mexico.

b 1 She's been to Brazil.
  2 They've been to Australia.
  3 They've been to Japan.
  4 He's been to Thailand.
  5 She's been to Canada.
  6 They've been to China.
  7 He's been to Malaysia.
  8 She's been to Argentina.

c 1 been 2 haven't 3 has 4 been
  5 hasn't 6 have 7 haven't 8 have

3 VOCABULARY

1 market 2 bank 3 theatre
4 supermarket 5 hospital
6 sports centre 7 chemist's
8 travel agent's

4 PRONUNCIATION

/ɒ/ country /ɜː/ really /e/ break
/k/ cinema /dʒ/ angry /h/ hour

---

1 VOCABULARY

a **Past participle:** broken, bought, driven,
  found, given, lost, made, run, written

b 1 bought 2 run 3 given
  4 written 5 broken 6 lost
  7 made 8 found 9 driven

2 PRONUNCIATION

/ɪ/ seen /ɔː/ found /e/ heard /ʌ/ got
/eɪ/ read /əʊ/ lost

3 GRAMMAR

a 1 didn't meet   5 started
  2 went   6 didn't see
  3 Have you read   7 haven't read
  4 has met   8 Did you go

b 1 Have you read 2 gave 3 did…like
  4 've read 5 Have…seen 6 took
  7 Was 8 didn't enjoy

---

4 READING

1 31st July 1965
2 six
3 English and Modern Languages
4 secretary and English teacher
5 to teach English
6 journalist
7 1993
8 in a café in Edinburgh
9 1997
10 millions

CAN YOU REMEMBER?

1 more 2 Would 3 coldest 4 well
5 been 6 Have

New English File Elementary online

 Grammar
Practise your grammar with exercises for each File.

 Vocabulary
Practise your vocabulary with exercises for each File.

 Pronunciation
Practise the sounds of English, and play sounds and word stress games.

 Audio Words
Listen to the words, learn them, and add your translation.

 Practical English
Listen to and learn phrases, and do 'spot the mistake' activities.

 Learning Record
Download the Study Link Learning Record (PDF, size 109 KB).

 Text Builder
Read and complete texts from the Student's Book.

 Weblinks
Links to websites for learning more about the topics in New English File Elementary.

 Games
Have some fun with our games – and learn English at the same time!

 Mini Phrasebook
Download two pages of Practical English for travelling. You can get this in colour (PDF, size 139 KB) or black and white (PDF, size 97 KB)

 Vocabulary Calendar
Write down and learn new words every month.
Download this month's calendar (PDF, size 32 KB)

Don't forget that New English File has a website for you at: www.oup.com/elt/englishfile/elementary
This helps you with:

- grammar
- vocabulary
- pronunciation
- Practical English
- listening
- reading
- writing
- spelling

Keep a record of what you've done with the
Study Link Learning Record.

File 1 **Study Link** learning record

Workbook

	✓	date
1A	✓	
1B	☑	10 October
1C	☑	24 October
1D	☐	
Practical English	☐	
	☐	

MultiROM

• Grammar Quiz 1	☐	
• Vocabulary Banks		
Numbers	☐	
Countries and nationalities	☐	
Common objects	☐	
• Practical English 1	☐	
• Audio – Workbook Question times 1A–D	☐	

Website www.oup.com/elt/englishfile
- Grammar – File 1 ☐
- Vocabulary Banks

…et, Oxford OX2 6DP

…s is a department of the University of Oxford.
…sity's objective of excellence in research, scholarship,
…y publishing worldwide in

…w York

…and Cape Town Dar es Salaam Hong Kong Karachi
…ala Lumpur Madrid Melbourne Mexico City Nairobi
New Delhi Shanghai Taipei Toronto

With offices in

Argentina Austria Brazil Chile Czech Republic France Greece
Guatemala Hungary Italy Japan Poland Portugal Singapore
South Korea Switzerland Thailand Turkey Ukraine Vietnam

OXFORD and OXFORD ENGLISH are registered trade marks of
Oxford University Press in the UK and in certain other countries

© Oxford University Press 2005

ISBN: 978 0 19 451824 6 (Pack)
ISBN: 978 0 19 451825 3 (Book)

Printed in China

ACKNOWLEDGEMENTS

Design and composition by: Stephen Strong

The Authors would like to thank all the teachers and students around the
world whose feedback has helped us to shape New English File. We would
also like to thank Russell and Anna, and Ben Silverstone for agreeing to be
interviewed, and Joaquin for the short story *It's written in the cards*. The
Authors would also like to thank all those at Oxford University Press (both
in Oxford and around the world), and the design team who have
contributed their skills and ideas to producing this course

*The Publisher and Authors would like to thank the following for their invaluable
feedback on the materials*: Beatriz Martin; Michael O'Brien; Lester Vaughan;
Tom Stutter; Wendy Armstrong; Javier Santos Asensi; Tim Banks; Brian
Brennan; Xosé Calvo; Javier Gesto; Susanna Di Gravio; Jane Hudson; Carlos
Leite; Norma Sheila Botelho; Paulo Pimenta Marques; Katarzyna Pawlowska;
Graham Rumbelow; Blanca Sanz; Yolanda Gomez; Ágnes Szigetvári; Judit
Gadanecné Szarka; Krzysztof Wierzba

Finally, very special thanks from Clive to María Angeles and from Christina
to Cristina for all their help and encouragement. Christina would also like
to thank her children Joaquin, Marco, and Krysia for their constant
inspiration

*The Publisher and Authors are grateful to those who have given permission to
reproduce the following extracts and adaptations of copyright material*: p.54 'A tale
of two Sydneys'. Reproduced by kind permission of Emma Nunn and Raoul
Sebastian; p.56 'tfi friday' by Harvey Marcus, *Marie Claire* October 2002 ©
Harvey Marcus/Marie Claire/IPC Syndication. Reproduced by permission;
p.67 'Friday Nights: Gosforth, Cumbria' by Stephen Bleach, *The Sunday Times*
28 October 2001 © NI Syndication London 2001. Reproduced by permission;
p.75 'My piece of pop history' by Andrew Holgate, *The Sunday Times* 6
October 2002 © NI Syndication London 2002. Reproduced by permission;
p.90 'Extreme Living' by Lucy Ash, *Eve Magazine* 2002. Reproduced by
permission of *Eve Magazine*

*The Publisher would like to thank the following for their kind permission to reproduce
photographs and other copyright material*: Alamy pp.52l (Andre Jenny),
61 (Gkphotography), 78r (Charlie Newham), 88d (TH Foto); Ann Scott
Associates p.97t; Car Photo Library pp.88h, 88i; Corbis UK Ltd. pp.53a
(Paul Almasy), 53b (Nik Wheeler), 53d (Araldo de Luca), 53e (Bettmann),
54t (Ray Juno), 58b (Horace Bristol), 58c (Hulton-Deutsch Collection), 58d
(Horace Bristol), 73l (Barry Lewis), 73r (Sergio Pitamitz), 78c (Szenes/Sygma),
78l (Ken Redding), 88b (Aaron Horowitz), 88c (Amos Nachoum), 88g
(John Conrad), 90c (Dean Conger), 90l (Wolfgang Kaehler), 90r (Balaguer
Alejandro/Sygma), 109l/112 (Bequest of Mrs. Benjamin Ogle Tayloe;
Collection of The Corcoran Gallery of Art), 109r/112 (Bettmann), 112b
(Robert Holmes); Getty Images pp.58f (Hulton Archive), 70tl (taxi); Gosforth
Hall Hotel pp.66, 66l; Hulton Archive/Getty Images p.58e; imageri.com
p.58a; Madame Tussauds p.70tr; Marie Claire/IPC Syndication/Kong Qingyan,
Frederico Mendes, Nikolai Ignatiev p.56; NASA p.88f (Reto Stockli/Alan
Nelson/Fritz Hasler); News International Syndication p.75l (Francesco
Guidicini/The Times); Oxford Scientific Films p.88a (David M Dennis);
Oxford University Press pp.94l, 94r, 95; Photofusion Picture Library p.68
(Nigel Goldsmith); Press Association p.148tc; Residence Tunis p.97br; Rex
Features pp.52r (Patsy Lynch), 53c (Stephen Meddle), 70b (Nils Jorgensen),
70bc, 71 (James D. Morgan), 75r (Crawford Brown), 89
(Nils Jorgensen), 99 (Rob Crandall), 109c/112; Ronald Grant Archive p.63t;
Robert Schirmer p.81b; Science Photo Library p.88e (US Geological Survey);
Ben Silverstone p.63b; Starwood Hotels & Resorts Worldwide, Inc. p.97bl;
WHSmith p.92; Zooid Pictures pp.64, 70tc (Dan Sinclair)

Illustrations by: Nick Baker: pp.64, 65, 69, 76, 85, 87, 104, 105, 123, 147;
Stephen Conlin: pp.106 (bridge/church), 152; Mark Duffin: pp.60, 72, 91,
106, 111, 129 (symbols), 151; Martha Gavin: pp.69 (flats), 88, 94, 95, 110,
113; Ellis Nadler: pp.54, 93, 150, pronunciation symbols; Robert Shadbolt:
pp.66, 67, 78, 79, 95 (actions), 133, 134; Colin Shelbourn: pp.77, 102, 106
(man), 134, 135; Annabel Wright: pp.82, 100, 101

Commissioned photography by: Mark Mason: pp.59, 76, 80, 85, 103, 106, 135,
153

Picture research by: Zooid Pictures

Illustrations commissioned by: Cathy Blackie

Commissioned photography organized by: Pippa MacNee

Thanks to: Paul Seligson and Carmen Dolz for the English Sounds Chart,
pp. 156,158

Workbook material by: Jane Hudson